Cairo

THE MOTHER OF THE WORLD

Herbert L. Smith

Cairo
The Mother of the World

Published by Wheatmark®
610 East Delano Street, Suite 104, Tucson, Arizona 85705 U.S.A.
www.wheatmark.com

ISBN: 978-1-60494-093-0
LCCN: 2008921006

TO GLENDA
Listener, editor, encourager, enabler.

Contents

Ramblings

I WENT TO CAIRO IN the mid-1990's and stayed for either three years or a lifetime. I can't be sure. In many ways I have never left, for Cairene life and thought have influenced my life and thought so completely that I am between two worlds; one world is my western roots and framework, the other the new and invasive world of Cairo that is jarringly different, intriguing, and inviting. I was and am captivated by Cairo, and am not at all sorry about it.

Cairo is a kaleidoscope of light and color. From the air, as I arrived for the first time, the city looked wearily drab and very much like the desert it sits on, but Cairo is no desert. Instead, a thriving, throbbing, turbulent city of tremendous contrasts and contradictions awaits on the shores of the Nile. Called "The Mother Of The World" by her citizenry, Cairo works, plays, lives, and plans the future as she recalls a former glory that is still vigorously present.

The ancient city of Memphis left a tiny remnant that is now contained in a small modern building just south of Cairo. A colossal statue of Ramses II, a beautiful alabaster sphinx, and a few smaller artifacts are all that remain. Some of the Pharaohs who once ruled there were buried in the pyramids at Giza, but almost everything except the pyramids themselves has disappeared over time, including the mummified remains of the Pharaohs. A later city, Fustat, founded in the seventh century, was located in the place where Cairo sits today. It is that city that became Al Quhira, the Victorious City, and the Mother of the World.

Today's Cairo is, in a word, indescribable, and no rhetoric will ever say it all, just as the city cannot truly contain itself. It is too large for containment, perhaps not in a physical sense, but the city seems to exceed in its own excess and has to be experienced for a while in order to be understood. There is too much of everything: poverty, traffic, noise, pollution, heat, sun and people. It is difficult to find a quiet spot for a much needed respite. Despite this, Cairo is completely engaging. From the first moment I walked into the scene, I was beguiled by the swirl of color and activity that surrounded everything I saw, and I quickly learned to love it that way. Cairo has a way of forcing everyone to enter wholly into the activity of the city and to experience as much of it as possible whenever one is among her people and involved in their life.

I went to Cairo to work, to be a mentor for Egyptian teachers who taught English in the Experimental Language Schools. There were several of these schools, and there were seven American teachers who inaugurated the mentor program.

Although I didn't teach any classes of my own, I spent most of my time in secondary school classrooms (they are never called "high schools") with Egyptian teachers, talking with their classes and teaching certain parts of the daily lessons. I also answered a great number of questions about the U.S., many about its most popular export to the Egyptian people—the girls especially—a soap opera, "The Bold And The Beautiful," that taught them that life in the U.S. was about beautiful people and places, and parties every night. While they feigned dislike for much of the soap, they were hooked, and that was obvious.

I had no experience with soap operas, and could not give any satisfaction about that kind of thing, but tried to tell the students that life in the U.S. for their counterparts was about staying home a lot in the evening and doing homework, watching TV, or talking to friends on the phone. Or all of those things. They would hardly believe me, but for an unusual reason; they couldn't imagine what it would be like to be able to connect to friends by phone so easily. In Egypt the phone service is poor at best, and often has so much static on the line that it is hard to hear, and even more often the phone simply doesn't work.

The most frequent question, however, was asked with anticipation: "What do secondary school students in the U.S. think about Egypt?" I told them that American students learned about the pyramids and other ancient monuments and some were very interested, but that most were concerned about their own lives in the U.S. and didn't think much about other places.

The next question was almost always the follow-up; "But what do they think about Cairo today?"

After trying to answer that diplomatically a few times, I decided to give them the truth. "They don't think about Cairo at all, because they know absolutely nothing about it." There was silence, then someone would say, "But we think about America every day." Of course they do. They see it glitzily displayed on TV.

I had responded to an ad in a newspaper about working in Egypt, which was how I finally got there. I did not know anything about modern Egypt myself, and did some research before I went, but that was not adequate. I found many surprises, and that was probably for the best, because the surprises were the things that caught my attention and made me appreciate what was really there. Clearly, it was the unexpected that made me love Cairo.

The ancient monuments, Pharonic times, and the deep history of the place is the great attraction to which the world responds, the reason for the tourist industry and all its associated parts in Egypt. The Nile Valley, filled with treasures beyond our imaginations, is an amazing place, and I have many favorite sites: Karnak Temples and the Valley of the Kings, the obelisk quarry at Aswan, Sakarra and the Giza plateau—especially the Sphinx—the Cairo Museum, and the Roman aqueduct that runs through the city toward the Khan al Khalili—these are the greatly magnificent remnants of other worlds in other times, but my real love goes primarily to some of the lesser places that tourists don't often find, and are not written about in guidebooks.

I once found a very old building in downtown Cairo when I went to a tailor shop on its upper floor. The building was old, by my standards anyway, probably somewhere between 250 and 300 years. Much of its interior had fallen to ruin. The stair case, a graceful, beautiful curving thing that led gently toward the top, was so worn that the stone steps had grooves where more than two centuries of feet had climbed, and the banisters and balustrades, missing some sections altogether, were of wood with no varnish remaining but were not splintered or rough. All the hands that had gripped them had worn them smooth.

The building was mostly empty and derelict. The tailor shop that remained on the top floor had been there for such a long time that no one knew for sure when it had been established. The proprietor had worked there for several decades, and he was only one in a line of tailors who had worked in that space. Once inside the door, the place was rather tidy, and there was glass in all the windows, electricity, and a small kitchen with a gas ring where tea was prepared many times every day. The floors were carpeted with one old carpet atop another, and there was even a vacuum cleaner, called a *hoover* in Arabic. A side hallway around the corner from the tailor shop entrance was partly closed off by a great pile of bird guano, and the broken windows throughout the building invited the wind as well as all the kinds of birds who made their home inside.

Most empty buildings in Cairo were filled with squatters. The peasants, called *felahin*, who came into the city for a better life, occupied every space that could be considered habitable, and some that did not seem to be, but they didn't live in *that* building. Maybe the flocks of birds kept them out, but the building was quiet, by Cairo standards, inside. Only the top floor and the stairs had any sign of activity. There were two or three areas that were used for businesses on the top, and customers regularly walked up and down the beautiful staircase. On the main floor, along the sidewalk, the empty windows sagged and some of the brickwork had fallen in heaps here and there. If I hadn't known that the tailor shop was there I would have never thought to look.

I found many old buildings in Cairo that occupied my attention on walks and set my imagination working. I saw wonderful houses that were at least five hundred years old. Modern plumbing pipes and electric wiring filled holes that were drilled through the thick stone, but, in most ways, the houses remained as they had been since they were built. Some had been "quarried" from the outer casings of the great pyramids, the large stones brought into the city and used for public buildings and houses in the time before records were kept. Most had originally been single family homes, but they filled up as families grew, and are now home to generations of grandparents and uncles and cousins. The same houses tend to be occupied by descendants of the people who built them, so there is a very strong connection with the past in those places.

There are mosques that are a thousand years old. Two of them are near The Citadel, and I walked through them one day with a Muslim friend. They are difficult to describe, their beauty so enhanced by their age that they seem poetic, solemnly grand, and a bit whimsical at the same time. The patterns in the mosaics and the carved stone are not recognizable because Muslims do not copy any living thing in their art, but the entire effect is of being in a leafy place with bowers and water and sky.

The Hussein Mosque, located near the Khan al Khalili, is old but refurbished. I walked through it with my friend Nadi, carrying shoes and talking, at times loudly, all the way. A mosque is not usually a hushed place. The walls were plain, and the floor covered with the most beautiful carpet I have seen. It was a deep red, with gold patterns around the sides and across the floor so that the immense place was divided visually, and the areas defined and more habitable. Mosques are sacred places, but the men who are there feel at home within their walls. They are places for living and thinking and reading as well as praying.

On that day we saw some groups of men sitting and talking, some reading, some keeping solitude, and even a group of mysticians in a far corner carrying on a dance that Nadi said would go on for hours; moving, turning, swaying, and jumping to the sound of their own voices keeping time, continuing in a trance for the duration. I wanted to see how the dance ended but we left because we couldn't stay for the hours it would take to come to a conclusion.

....

Many people in the Middle East have little concept of maintenance. They do not repaint or repair their houses easily, and if something goes wrong with equipment they tend to wait until they can replace it, or find some way to get something else to use. Cars are a noted exception, but they hardly keep up their cars the way we do in the U. S. They are not obsessed with them, anyway.

I heard at times about someone getting a "new" house. I learned that they meant that those people were repainting, repairing, and refurnishing the space that they already lived in, and so it would be renewed. In that sense, their house was a "new" once every twenty or thirty years.

I had some interesting experiences with Egyptian attempts at maintenance at my house, a very large just-built flat on the fifteenth floor of a twenty story residential building.

Very soon after I moved in, I got up one morning to get ready for school and there was no water. I knew that there were three different water pumps on my side of the building, and that my kitchen and both bathrooms (I lived in luxury by Egyptian standards) were all on different pumps. There was no water in any of the pipes, so I called the owner of the flat to ask what I could do about the situation. She was not happy. She told me that if I was not satisfied we could tear up the lease agreement and she would find another tenant. After a short discussion, I could see that I was over-reacting, so I apologized for calling her so early and went into the kitchen for the bottles of water I used for drinking, emptied most of them into the bathtub, and was able to get myself off to school in time.

The water pumps, I learned later, were turned off in the entire building because one had burned out, and the maintenance people, not knowing what to do, had turned them all off so that the system would not be overworked. This reasoning did not make sense to me because the pumps were all separate, but I know that it made perfect sense to the maintenance men.

One other event is even more telling. There are two elevators in the building, one that stops on odd numbered floors, and one for the even numbered. They are side by side on the ground floor, and if mine was in use I could always get into the other and ride up to the sixteenth floor and walk down. Problems came when the electricity was off—which happened almost every day for about an hour—and the elevators didn't work at all. In order to go out I had to walk down all the fifteen floors, (and often up as well) and that was not easy because the lights were off, too. The stairwell was very dark until I got close enough to the bottom to see by the light coming through the entrance.

One day I noticed a sign in the elevator saying that it would be painted the following day. The next morning I went into the passage and pushed the button. The lights in the stairway were on, but the elevator didn't respond. Then I remembered the notice and went down one flight to get the elevator on the next, even numbered floor. There was no response.

In disbelief I walked down the to the ground floor and looked at the elevators. Painters were working. They were painting *both* elevators at the same time, and everybody had to walk up as well as down for two days because the paint took more than twenty four hours to dry.

....

An aspect of Cairene life that concerns many people is the carpet industry. It is said that children are enslaved in the carpet factories and used for long hours to make carpets. Many people have decided to boycott the carpet industry for that reason. One evening at about nine, I visited a carpet shop and saw a number of children there, not obviously working, but playing among the carpets that a few men were sewing. The workshop was open until about midnight, as was usual for such businesses in Egypt. They made entirely hand-made carpets there, and I didn't see a loom in the entire place. They all seemed to be stitched together in some way.

The carpets hung from cables that were fastened to tracks in the ceiling, and the children ran between the carpets, flapping the corners as they played a game of tag. They were noisy and squealing, but when one of the men called, two children came up and took the bottom of the carpet to pull it flatter so he could stitch a pattern into the very bottom edge. Other children stopped at times to place a few stitches into the very lowest part of the carpets themselves.

In my opinion, these children were not enslaved, although some in other factories may be, but were carefree and happy as they jostled in and out among the hanging carpets. I suspect that most factories use child labor in much the same way. Egyptians seem to understand that children need frolic and fun in order to do a good job at the tasks they are given.

I have often noticed the number of toy stores in Cairo. Every other block seems to have a store stuffed with stuffed animals, games, tricycles, balls; everything you can imagine would be available there. These toys are, of course, for families who can afford such luxuries for their children, but there must be lots of families who buy them, and there must be lots of happy children in Cairo, playing with the toys, enjoying the advantages of a middle class childhood. I noticed customers coming and going in the shops I passed, buying presents for birthdays, special holidays, and even Christmas gifts. Some Muslims celebrate Christmas in an indirect way.

One Saturday morning in early January I went to a big hotel near my house for coffee and was surprised to see a long line of kiddies along with their mothers, waiting in the hallway outside a large ballroom. I looked through the open door and was even more surprised to find a huge throne-chair with Santa Claus resplendent upon it, a child in his lap.

I looked back at the line. The young mothers there were mostly Muslim because they wore carefully arranged headscarves, which Christian women do not wear, and they had brought their children to see Santa and to pose for a picture or two with him.

I asked a friend about this and he told me that Muslims don't celebrate Christmas exactly, but they do believe that Jesus was a prophet, and so the day to honor his birthday is popular with young families who have children. It's a good excuse to give presents.

....

Although sometimes difficult to see, there is a daily schedule of life in Egypt—a rhythm. As in any very hot country, Egyptians take advantage of the night hours, when the sun is gone and the air is a bit cooler, to do much of their work. Businesses open in the morning at about nine, and close for the afternoon at one or two. They will reopen at six or six thirty, and business goes on until perhaps ten or later. The evening is the favorite time for families to go out visiting each other, and they tend to stay up very late.

Sleep is in two shifts; in the afternoon after a substantial meal has been eaten, and in the night between one or two a.m. until seven or eight, when they get up to do their daytime work. The total sleep time per day is usually eight hours or a little more, and being divided into two parts provides rest when they begin to get tired. I learned to use this sleep pattern and prefer it to the western world's sleeping only at night.

Many times I have received a phone call at about midnight from a friend wanting to drop by while he was in the neighborhood. I always said yes, even if, western fashion, I was already in bed.

Schools are a different matter for time scheduling. Classes begin at eight thirty, or are at least scheduled for that time, and end at about one thirty so that students can go home to eat and sleep. Many students, and teachers as well, come late and leave early every day. In the western world where we are taught that time discipline is important, we cannot accept this apparently irresponsible behavior. In the Egyptian world it is normal for everyone to be tolerant toward these kinds of things, but intolerant when it comes to western acceptance of many other behaviors, especially those dealing with male and female relationships.

There is, however, some sort of hidden line that no one should cross, even if some things are tolerated. A student who comes to school too late will usually find the gate locked, and no one admitted or allowed out until the gate is unlocked by a servant. A teacher who misses too many days or always arrives too late will be shunned by some of the other faculty members in order to learn the lessons of acceptable behavior in these matters. Those kinds of nuances are almost impossible to be learned or understood by anyone who comes into the situation as a foreign visitor, which I always was, no matter how much time we spent working together. I was not permanent, as we all knew.

I was told that school started at eight a.m. for the faculty and that classes began at eight thirty, and for the first few days I was there at or before eight. No one else came until about nine, not even the principal of the school or the head of the department, and no students were yet to be seen. I was alone with the servants who were still sweeping and preparing for the day. After a few days I started going to work at about eight forty five, fearing that any day everyone else would be there and I would be considered late, but that never happened. Eight a. m. was just a suggestion for a starting time. About nine was the reality.

In most matters, Egyptians are causal about time. A little late is not a bad thing, and few are upset if meetings or business lasts longer than usual. Work can be done at a different pace than in other parts of the world, and life is generally a take-it-as-it-comes proposition. One day at the school I was looking out the window at a neighboring university building that was being renewed. I had seen workers coming and going, but now I saw a lot of men congregated on the top floor, directly over the wall from where I stood. They had a large, heavy looking sledge hammer, and the men lined up, I would guess ten or twelve of them, and one by one they swung the hammer onto the floor. They were breaking the concrete. That method seemed a great solution for work that could become very tiring if only two or three were taking turns, but with the large group they could take a mighty swing and rest quite awhile before taking another. That is the Egyptian way. Do the work, but plan an efficient way to do it that is less tiring than working alone.

Egyptian farmers who still work the fields do so on tiny patches of land that most Americans would find totally inadequate. Yet they raise crops, alternating with tomatoes and beans, or perhaps carrots and a different vining crop, or sweet potatoes, a staple of Egyptian "snack" diet. The soil stays in good condition, largely because it is fed by underground water that comes from the Nile and is rich in nutrients. The farmers also provide for families. If the family is large they might work two or three patches of land, and they are able to live, although meagerly, on the proceeds they get when their produce is sold in Cairo.

They tend to sell the produce themselves, hauling it to the street markets by donkey cart, arriving early in the morning and staying until late if they haven't sold everything. Sometimes, other entrepreneurs buy the sweet potatoes, bake them in small ovens brought along in donkey carts, and sell them on the street. The carts are a common sight around schools, where the students buy the hot, sweet snack on their way home. The smoky odor is very alluring and I have been tempted to buy one, but the warning, "Don't ever eat street food!" that came from other westerners living in Cairo, prevented me.

I didn't eat street food, but I still developed a serious illness that is more or less endemic in Egypt—hepatitis. It was the A type, and although I wasn't sick very long, it did, in a manner of speaking, take a lot out of me. I stayed home a few days, but probably went back too soon because at the time I didn't know what the illness was. I thought I just had a stomach upset and didn't eat for awhile because nothing agreed with me. Later I discovered, on the advice of a friend whose husband and children had all suffered through the disease, exactly what the symptoms were, and went to a doctor to confirm what I thought. By that time the infectious state was past. Then I learned that I wasn't the only person at my school who had hepatitis. Three other teachers were diagnosed at about the same time. I think the sickness may have been caused by some less than sanitary conditions with the tea and coffee glasses at school which were rather like communal cups. The tea and coffee were very hot, often too hot to handle. (I learned to pick the glasses up by holding the bottom edge and the upper rim carefully.) I had believed that the heat would kill any germs, but that was not the case. Anyway, very few people live in Egypt for any length of time without getting sick from *something*, and my something was hepatitis A.

Learning how to live in Cairo was always interesting. Sometimes it was a challenge to anticipate what might happen as a result of an action I might—or might not—take. One challenge was paying my electric bill. The bill itself was rather small, usually less than ten dollars every month, about thirty five Egyptian Pounds. There were three flats on the fifteenth floor; mine, on the north side, was the largest, and the other two were on the southeast and southwest. The man who came to collect the electric bills (there is no postal delivery system in Cairo) asked me to collect from my two neighbors for him, but I refused, having been warned about such schemes. I would end up paying for all the flats on the fifteenth floor because the neighbors would refuse to pay me. No receipts were ever issued.

A few days after I told him that I wouldn't collect from my neighbors, I came home to find my house dark. The electricity had been turned off. I tried to think like an Egyptian, and managed to succeed that one time. In the hall, just beside my door, were two boxes that held the fuses for my flat. These fuses were huge, about three inches wide, with a large screw-in base. I looked in the boxes and they were both empty. I remembered that the flat below mine was currently unoccupied, so went downstairs, opened the fuse boxes and removed the fuses. I put them into my boxes, the electricity came on, and I never had another problem with the electric man.

Another notable incident was the result of my visit to Jerusalem. Although the border was open between the two countries, Egyptians did not trust the Israelis. Many of my friends took serious exception to my plan to go to Israel one year during the semester break. I decided to go by bus because I wanted to see the land, to ferry across the Suez canal, and especially to see North Sinai. Israel had returned it to Egypt following a short war, which the Egyptians claimed as a victory.

I made the mistake, however, of making arrangements by telephone from my flat. I called the hotel in Jerusalem from my own phone. My telephone service had been upgraded by the owner of the flat because she knew that I wanted to call the U.S. often. I got a new, clear line about two months after moving there, and was unusually fortunate to have it. I used the line to call many places in the U.S., but made a serious mistake in placing a call to Jerusalem.

Everything was fine until I returned from the trip. By then my telephone had been returned to the old, noisy line, but with an addition. I had a listener. Whenever I picked up the phone I heard small sounds in the distance, and often there were voices as well. I wondered if my line had gotten crossed with another, but when I talked to the owner of the flat she told me that I must be the object of government surveillance—a phone tap.

I called and talked to friends, always with the listener. I tried to call the U.S. but the static was so bad I couldn't hear. I had to do something, so I talked to the listener. For several days I would pick up the phone and speak directly to whoever was listening. I spoke harshly at first, but finally decided that friendliness might get more results, so I started chatting and asking about how he was (no women would ever be allowed to do that kind of work) and one day when he coughed I asked him, quite sympathetically, if he was sick. Simple things like that befuddled the listener, and sometimes when I spoke with friendliness and interest, he would answer me. Once we even had a brief conversation. It was both fun and infuriating, but didn't accomplish my purpose.

A friend went to the heart of the problem. He went to the telephone company office, not far from the school where I worked, and complained that he couldn't reach me when he tried to call. Then other friends began to do the same thing, and on some days three or four people went to complain. Finally, the owner of the flat went in to complain. In less than a week I had my good line restored and lost the listener.

In Arab countries, as in most places in the world, it's the squeaky wheel that gets the grease.

The Impossible City

THE MODERN CITY OF Cairo has all the problems of any over populated city, and more. Cairo is unique. It has been called the noisiest city in the world, and may well be. The city has been named by some the dirtiest, but that is debatable, and is currently listed as perhaps the most polluted anywhere. That could be true as well.

Cairo is divided into two governates: Cairo proper on the eastern side of the Nile, and Giza on the west. In the past, population counts have been divided between the governates, and Cairo has been considered much smaller than the entire urban area actually was. Of course, the governates have been around for a long time, but it is still convenient to consider only the Cairo half whenever anyone suggests that the city has become an "impossible", overly crowded place.

Attempts at true estimates of the city's population run from less than fifteen million up to more than twenty million, but the lower estimates do not take into account the vast number of felahin who come in by day, and the crowds who settle permanently every year, estimated by the Egyptian government to be one thousand people per day. Cairo is growing. It is the largest city in Africa, and in at least one list is named the seventh largest city in the world.

Called an impossible city by some of its own citizens due to overcrowding, pollution of the air and water, heat and dust, noise, the squatter invasion, sanitation difficulties, and monumental traffic, Cairo is also filled with decaying buildings, moldering walls and gardens, and lack of sanitation due to the number of people who live on the streets or in makeshift lean-tos against the walls that line the streets. Everything adds up to a city that can't possibly exist as it is, but does. Cairenes are somewhat proud of this, and I must admit that I am, too.

This assessment is in no way a callous or cavalier attitude toward the millions of people who have no home, but is an assertion that those people, along with all the rest, have found a better life there than in the villages and towns in upper Egypt, and that they, too, benefit from the life that Cairo offers. They can have better nourishment, at least *some* modern healthcare, and, in many cases, a better place to live than in the situations they have fled from. Even beggars in Cairo are better off than beggars in upper Egypt.

There are many distractions, difficulties to overcome, and negatives for anyone who tries to live there, whether a Cairene or an expatriate, but for those of us who love the city, these are bearable and even, in some cases, add to the attraction. One certainty is that life in Cairo is not as easy as life in a western city for those whose cultural roots are from the west, but the compensations are great and at times overwhelmingly beautiful.

One of my first experiences in Cairo was a trip to *borg al qahira;* Cairo Tower, a newish symbol of Cairo, sixty-six stories tall, on the island of Zamalek in what was once the British enclave. A young teacher from school came to pick me up at the hotel where I was living temporarily, and we drove there in his tiny Fiat. The afternoon was still hot, and the sun was quite a way from setting when we rode the elevator to the top and stepped out onto the observation platform.

The air was cooler there, and a strong breeze was blowing from the west. Cairo tower is a round tower that looks slender from a distance, but when I was there, on top, it seemed to enlarge to become big enough for more people than I thought possible to walk around on the observation deck. Fahim, the teacher I was with, pointed out various places of interest in the city, but I could never remember much from that day; being too soon to be able to assimilate much information about a place that was so immense. I only looked, and appreciated. I saw the open playing fields of Zamalek, some of the major roadways, the great path of the Nile passing close to the lawns that surrounded the tower, and the island of Manial (or Roda) to the south. I saw the great bridges, big hotels, and other large buildings in the distance, but didn't recognize any of them yet.

Months later I went back to the tower with another friend. I looked at things differently then, knowing where to look and what to look for. I found my house after much searching through a telescope. Just one side of the building was open to view from where I stood, not even the side that my flat was on, but I could recognize the place and its neighbor, Mustashfa ibn sina, Brothers of Sinai hospital, and felt at home.

Immediately after my first trip to borg al qahira I was involved in my first auto accident in Cairo. Several followed, but the first was the only one that caused any injury. When a large new car came through the intersection and hit the front end of Fahim's Fiat, he got out to talk to the driver. I waited in the car, rubbing my knee that had gotten a hard bump, not wanting to get involved in an Egyptian matter. After a few minutes, Fahim came to the door and asked me to talk to the owner of the car, a woman who had just arrived on the scene in another car. "She speaks English well," he told me, "and she wants to talk to you."

Reluctant to get involved, I got out and approached her. She introduced herself without asking my name and asked how the accident occurred. "Your driver was driving too fast," I told her, "and he hit this car on the left front end. From the position of the place where he hit us, you can see that we were in the intersection first." She looked, said *"ensha'allah"*, and turned to Fahim. She spoke in Arabic for a moment and then got into her car and was driven away.

"It's over," Fahim told me. "She decided not to make me pay."

"How could she make you pay? Her driver was at fault." I protested.

"You're in Egypt now" Fahim responded. "Here the rich person is compensated by the poor person in cases like these. Rich people expect to get away with things. She wanted me to pay for her damages, but I asked her to talk to you first."

There was no police presence at all. The police rarely get into traffic situations, even if someone is injured or killed in an accident. *"Ensha'allah"* is the attitude. Ensha'allah means "as God wills."

The police are interesting in Cairo. Although there are government offices for, or general supervision of, police, it is difficult to comprehend exactly who is in charge and what the guiding principles of the police department are. I speak, not from western culture or expectation, but from the frustration that the native Cairenes I know often feel.

Decades ago, an old hotel called the Shepheard's was a major stop for English speaking tourists in Cairo. The venerable hotel, beloved by the expats who lived in the city, was their meeting place and home to a belly dancing show that was very popular among tourists and expats alike. That belly dancing show became the undoing of the Shepheard's Hotel.

One night in 1952, after several days of rioting, ironically carried out by the police who were trained to control riots—the riot police— they marched on the Shepheard's and torched it, ostensibly because of the belly dancing that went on there, counter to their strong Islamic beliefs. The hotel burned to the ground. Everyone was able to escape because the progress of the torching party was well publicized at it came through the city, but the hotel was gone. A new hotel was built, the second incarnation of The Shepheard's Hotel, but the Victorian edifice was no more.

The riot police burned other hotels as well in their passionate protest, and the riot of the riot police has became a part of the ironic history of Cairo.

Traffic police are another matter; they stand in the center of the most heavily trafficked midans in Cairo and, with a wave of a hand, control the progress of a few hundred cars at any particular moment. They appear to be unruffled by all the noise and honking and the tag-playing drivers who surround them. They blow their whistles and move their arms in elegant motion, proud to be at the center of things in the city. Drivers are long accustomed to their presence, and most obey the signals that the officers give them.

There is another kind of traffic policeman, however. He is the one who issues tickets for various infractions of traffic laws. At least, that is his supposed purpose, but these policemen are said to be governed by a quota system. They are told that each officer must gather a certain amount of money from traffic fines that day, and they set out to do exactly that. A taxi driver I know (he operates a guide service that I hired a few times to take visiting friends around the city) told me that he had gotten three tickets in one day, that he had paid two, but protested the third as a little too much. The tickets were not issued to him for breaking laws, but he happened to be in the wrong place at the wrong time. He was pulled over and given a ticket by one policeman, for speeding, he was told, but it is almost impossible to speed in Cairo. The traffic is so heavy that they have gridlock much of the time, and only a trickle of the cars get through when there is an opening. Most have to wait for a long time to go through a crowded street or intersection. After his first ticket, he drove a short distance and was stopped again, and fined again, for speeding. He didn't protest. He told me that every driver expects to have a certain number of tickets each year, and that is figured into the cost of doing business.

On the third ticket, which was given to him later that day, he did protest at the court when he went to pay, and the judge cleared the third ticket for him. He reasoned that the driver had been hit too hard already, and should not have an undue burden of paying for three tickets in one day.

The Nile has seven bridges that form the only crossings between Giza and Cairo. All these bridges are filled to capacity most of the time, day and night. There are long lines of cars and buses, donkey carts, and even camel herds waiting to cross them. The leading cars and taxis tend to crowd together, blocking all the lanes of the approaches to the bridge while they awaited the signal to cross. This creates a terrible rush onto the bridge as cars, especially taxis, attempt to beat each other across the river. This is a constant activity at both ends of the bridges and is only controlled, and that at a minimum, by the presence of traffic policemen.

....

An American friend told me once that "nothing is ever discarded" in Cairo. She was referring to technology, and that certainly seems to apply. There are Pharonic era water wheels that continue to be used. They dip into a canal or the river and bring the water up and over, to spill into a smaller canal that waters a farmer's land.

Multi-storied buildings are built with a scaffold made of tree limbs fastened together with heavy ropes. They go right up to the top of the buildings, twenty or more floors. Crude handmade ladders connect the floors until stairways are made, sometimes months after construction begins. The limbs for the ladders and scaffolds are old and worn smooth from use, but the visual effect, after the initial surprise wears off, is that of a piece of folk art.

The donkey cart and versions of it are perhaps the most frequent reminder that nothing ever goes out of use in Cairo. Farmers bring in produce to sell in the street markets on large carts. They also bring their families along at times, riding on top of the load of vegetables and whatever else they plan to sell. They spend their day in the city, returning to the delta at night with the money they have been paid for their efforts.

Carts are used by vendors; some selling reed furniture or clothing or carpets and rugs, but many vendors sell food. Some street food is appealing. It smells very good, and seems like a great opportunity, but I have been warned most seriously to stay away, and I know why. One day while walking near my house I saw a man on his knees, working directly on the street. He had placed a large circle of flour in a ring, and was adding water and egg and oil to it to make into a dough from which he would bake flatbread in the oven he hauled along in his donkey cart. The street was unwashed, as was the man, and I stood there watching incredulously. I knew that feral dogs haunted the streets at night, that thousands of dirty shoes passed over that place every day, and that people who lived nearby in squatter tents dumped their chamber pots along the street every morning. The street was swept by crews with short handled brooms, but that was not the same as a good washing. There was never any rain, so years of dirt and disease had the opportunity to accumulate. I also knew that people would come to his cart and buy the bread once it was baked, and a family would share it at a meal later in the day.

....

I liked to go to a coffee shop called Groppi's in downtown Cairo. I didn't like it for the food, although that wasn't really too bad, but because of its living history. Groppi's is an old place that had been refurbished in the 1930's with metal tables and chairs, and has never been touched again. The furniture was bent and rusted in places, and the floor was worn and uneven. The windows were not quite clean, and once there was water gushing from the ceiling in the back of the room. Truly gushing. Water flowed out across the floor in the opposite direction from the entrance while customers were being served in the rest of the place. The problem area was roped off. When I went back a couple of months later everything was the same, except for the gushing water. It no longer flowed, but there had been no attempt to repair the ceiling or the floor in that area, which was still roped off. It may be still in that condition, for all I know.

I met a man there who told me that his name was Miguel. He saw me come in, and soon was at my table asking if we could chat. I agreed, somewhat tentatively, and he sat down and started into his story. He was Brazilian, he said, and was traveling around Europe when he got the idea to come see Egypt. He was affable, easy to talk to, and interesting. After a few subtle hints that he was involved in some sort of criminal activity, he told me that he was actually in Cairo hiding from the law, and that he was there on an Italian passport. He showed me his passport, and added that he had quite a number of others hidden among his things.

He was not Egyptian, I knew. His speech was accented with what I thought was Spanish, but could have been Portuguese. I listened and smiled and told him just a little about myself, still fairly comfortable with him but not sure what he wanted. So I waited, drinking coffee and eating some chocolate cake.

He said he came there every afternoon "for something to do" because he was so bored in Cairo. I agreed to meet him there on the weekend, and I did.

Miguel was waiting for me when I got to Groppi's, and after exchanging the pleasantries of "how are you" and so on, he got into more of his story. He told me that he was actually a hit man—a hired assassin—and that he had done a job recently in a South American country, where he had shot his mark, but also had to shoot another innocent man who had seen what happened. He was sorry about that. He described the whole thing in quiet detail, and I responded in as cavalier a manner as I could, under the circumstances.

We talked about this for awhile, then the conversation turned to other things, and he told me a few more incidents in his career. By that time it was growing late, so I was able to get away without indicating how upset he had made me, and what a terrible judge of character I was. Not that I believed him, but to be so caught off-guard by an experienced pathological liar—if he was that instead of an assassin—is rather discomfitting. I don't recall ever going back to Groppi's.

....

I often passed a small produce shop near the school where I worked. It was in the bottom of a tall building, in a semibasement room. Some narrow cement stairs led down to a door that was always open. There were a few vegetables sitting on tables on the street level, but they were wilted and tired looking. I decided one day that I would go into the shop to see if there was anything worthwhile there. The shop was a tiny place, with just one door and no windows.

After I got through the door I saw the proprietor in the dim light, a rather burly man of indeterminate age wearing a dirty white galabeya and a turban. He greeted me in Arabic and English, and asked me, cordially enough, what I was looking for. I told him that I was just looking over his selection of vegetables, and he started talking about the various things he had in the store.

I looked at the carrots and strawberries and eggplant, but they were all past any imaginary expiration date that might have applied, so after a short while I said "*Shukron*" and started to leave. He stood in the doorway, barring my way, and told me that I had to buy something. His shop wasn't for browsing, he told me. I had to buy something once I came inside.

To say that I was incensed would be mild. I walked up to him and nearly lifted him as I pushed and shouted, "No! I'm going!" He gave way and I went up the stairs as fast as I could. I was glad to be free of the place and its proprietor. But I hadn't entirely escaped his wrath.

After I had walked about two blocks up the street I felt something pull on my hand, and as I looked around, a small boy darted away down the street. He had left something in my hand. I looked again—it was a one pound note.

Later I asked an Egyptian friend about the incident, and he told me that it was an ultimate insult among Arabs. If someone attempted to make a fool of another in a financial deal, the "victim" would often respond with a token of a small amount of money given to the perpetrator. I found this rather comical given the circumstances, and enjoyed a sweet roll at a local bakery with the money.

....

About a week after I had arrived in Cairo I had become accustomed to living in the hotel and was sleeping better. Then one night I heard loud, pounding music coming from the bar on the top floor. The music continued, sounding very much like a huge party with a DJ who had booming speakers, and I waited for things to quiet down. Sometime after midnight, early by Egyptian standards, I called the desk to complain. They told me that the noise wasn't coming from the hotel at all, but from a rooftop wedding party just down the street. I went out and took a good look, and there it was, blaring into the night.

    I soon learned that this was common in Egypt, in all the Middle East in fact, and that everyone is entitled to celebrate until dawn for a wedding. The celebration included the shrill yelping cries of joy, called ululation, from the women, which sounded very strange to my ears. There was also the throbbing of the drums over the speakers, and the frequent commentary by the DJ and others. Mostly, I remember the shrill cries of jubilation. I could never get used to that sound in all the time I lived in Egypt.

    I slept very little that night, but finally drifted off toward dawn, when the party stated to slow down. After I knew people better, I asked a friend about the custom. "It is their right," he said. "They have a right to make merry when they can." I rather dimly understood the necessity of that kind of revelry at a wedding, but the seemingly pumped up euphoria has always eluded complete understanding. I have to agree that festivity is in order for the occasion, but have never been able to understand how keeping an entire neighborhood awake all night is tantamount to celebration.

....

In most of the world, the penthouse at the top of a building is prized residential space. This is not the usual case in Cairo.

Traditionally in the Middle East, the rooftop of a building is a storage and service area, the place where broken furniture awaits repair, clothes are dried on lines, servants sleep in small huts, cast-offs are stored, and any uncertain thing that may be of some use later is kept. In rural areas, animal feed and hay are also kept on top of the houses.

The roofs of tall buildings in cities are no exemption to this cultural habit, and the rooftop is where the felahin maintain a more or less permanent foothold in the city. They are not squatters there, but have legitimate structures to live in, and are the servants of the people who live in the beautiful flats below them.

In the building where I lived, the felahin were not allowed to use the elevators and so had to walk all twenty floors to go in and out, but the rooftop was home to them and their families. I have no idea how many. Some of the *bowabs* (as in *bow* and arrow)—porters—who worked in the building were living on top, and it is likely that their cousins and other relatives who moved to Cairo might have constructed their own enclosures on the roof as well. The felahin are tribal, from small villages along the river, and remain tribal after they relocate to the city.

The head bowab and his family lived in some small rooms just off the entrance lobby of the building. It was this bowab who was paid every month by all the tenants, and his relatives who worked for him were paid when he sent them to a flat in response to a call for some errand or other kind of job. I kept at least one bowab fairly busy getting cases of drinking water and carrying them up the fifteen flights to my house. I tended to pay well, so my requests were always answered promptly.

The bowabs are also the security men for their building, and they have developed a tight surveillance system. One or more always sat outside the front door at a small desk until very late at night. I was told they actually kept a record of who left, and when, the time they returned, and everyone who came into the building to visit as well as which flat they visited. When I passed their table there was rarely any sign of record keeping, but once in awhile I could see a small note-book lying there at the ready. I assumed that the notebook was the place where all the information was stored.

Squatters are a very visible part of Cairo There are families of squatters living in any building that is under construction until it is near completion and they are forced out. They set up tent-like walls for privacy and climb up a system of ladders to all the floors of an unfinished site. When the building is ready for interior walls, there aren't many squatters left to send away. Most have already found an-other new building to move into. This does not mean that squatters are uprooted every month or so. Many of the buildings that were al-ready partially completed when I moved to my house were still in about the same condition when I left three years later.

Squatters also live along many of the streets in the city. They put up lean-tos against the walls that surround houses and buildings, and live on the street. I have seen some lean-tos very near the building I lived in, and one of them, which seemed to have been there for many years, even had a second floor with a partly open balcony facing the street. The felahin tend to live by the strict Islamic code, so women are rarely if ever seen, but are hidden away inside their houses or lean-tos, only getting outside in an enclosed space, if it exists.

I have seen felahin living in some very unlikely places. There is a pedestrian bridge across a very busy street in the heart of Islam-ic Cairo, and the bridge is lined with carpet and canvas dwellings where squatters live above the noise and pollution of the street. There is barely room most of the time for pedestrians to get across.

One of the largest populations of squatters live in the two Muslim cemeteries that lie just below the Mukkotam Hills, "The Cities of the Dead," on the eastern side of the city. The cemeteries are filled with miniature houses of stone and marble that are built over the tombs, and these houses, although small, provide shelter for families, often for generations of families. The cemetery dwellers make cooking fires in the sandy avenues between the tombs, and children play in and around the avenues.

The Cities of the Dead have become a tourist attraction, so busloads of people who are curious or fascinated with these cemetery dwellers come by to take a look and to take pictures of the unfortunates. No one knows how many people live there, but the general belief is that these cemeteries are rather populous, both above and below ground. These felahin, however, are not concerned about their living situation. They are happy to find a better quality of life among the tombs.

....

Walking across a street in Cairo is a combination of science and artful dodging. It is a difficult thing to do in most cases, especially when crossing a major street; Sharia Dokki, for example.

The place where I walked across Sharia Dokki every school day was directly opposite the entrance lane to the school where I worked. The lane is a one-way single track with high walls, a sandy stretch of about three city blocks that has no cross streets until one comes to the far end. There the lane is stopped by a gate and traffic has to turn right or go through. The school is straight on through the gate, so I had no choice but to go down that way.

Major streets have clearly marked traffic lanes, usually two or three in each direction, but drivers pay no attention to lane markings. A two lane direction usually has three cars traveling abreast along its entire distance, and wider streets have as many cars as can be squeezed into them. One-way streets, while clearly marked, mean nothing to the Cairene. They do present a bit more challenge, however. The signs and arrows are considered mere suggestions, and cars are always threading through in the opposite direction. Egyptians seem to believe that there is no need to go out of the way to drive down another street when the place they want to go is at the end of the street they are facing into, even if it is one-way in the opposite direction. The only thing that will stop them from driving the wrong way is a traffic policeman directing the flow of cars.

I stood watching the other pedestrians, mostly students, who waited to cross Sharia Dokki on my first day to make the attempt. I watched as they waded out between the moving cars, stepping back as a car approached but did not stop, almost getting hit by another that came up behind. It looked like a game of chicken, and really was, for I learned to step boldly out in front of cars, that, although they were going slowly because of the congestion, were not wanting to stop for anyone.

It took some time, and I usually crossed when someone else was right beside me, hoping that two pedestrians would make the drivers more willing. Finally, I took the plunge alone, and stepped in front of a car that was about ten feet away. That's a long distance for one car to follow another in Cairo. I stepped out and the car stopped. I waited a moment and when I saw the opportunity, stepped in front of the next car, and when I got to the center, turned my attention the opposite direction and kept moving across until I had reached the other side. That was not an easy thing to do, but as I gained experience I developed the confidence to cross other, even busier, streets as well.

Cairenes tend to pay scant attention to traffic signs and lights, but they do pay attention to traffic policemen. If a policeman is in the center of an intersection, directing traffic, everyone obeys him and things are much smoother. If he stops traffic to allow pedestrians to cross, all the drivers wait, fuming, until he signals for them to go again. It is far safer to cross streets where a policeman controls the flow of traffic, but they are found at only a small percentage of the corners in Cairo, places that are so crowded with cars and people on foot that it would be near suicide to try to walk across the intersection without help.

....

The Mugamma is a name that causes fear to rise in the minds of most Cairenes. The Mugamma is the mega-government building in Cairo, at the southern end of Midan Tahrir. Mugamma is Arabic for "together"—most of the bureaucratic governmental offices are in one building, "together"—implying that work can be completed more readily at an easy to reach location in the heart of the city.

The Mugamma is twenty stories tall, shaped in a somewhat triangular fashion, and as formidably grey-cement-looking as any government building can be. This is the place, where, according to modern folktales, applications, forms, plans, memos, and assorted other paperwork goes to die. The shouting and tears that take place within its cavernous belly are too numerous to be believed, and idle office workers have been too numerous to make the place of much use to the public.

Some years ago a study was done on what actually goes on there, and the result showed that office workers in that building worked an average of sixteen minutes a day. At the time I lived in Cairo, employment laws protected the worker, even under extreme conditions. No one could be fired, and that created a situation that was untenable. That may have been a "loophole" in the law when it was made, but that loophole was not plugged until 2003, and a great number of workers did not work at their jobs—or even go to the workplace very often—and they were still paid.

The result was that wages were very low, extremely low, for workers, and although they couldn't legally accept other work until their current job ended by voluntary resignation, they were guaranteed a small income. Employers and even the government found creative ways to work around the law and they did, but paying for all the people who never showed up was costly.

There were two payment systems in Egypt for that reason. There was the required wage, which was equivalent to about $30 per month or less, and then there was the bonus. People who came to work every workday in the month for the normal number of hours qualified for the bonus, which was many times higher than the basic wage for the job. The bonus still was not enough to live on, however, so many people worked a second and even a third job, — an under the table job, that is — in order to be able to live. I know of a young man, just out of the university, who worked as a librarian in a university library, and as a barber in a shop near me. I met him there, and he always cut my hair because he was the only one who spoke English. He had a third job, but whatever it was I did not know. He seemed reluctant to talk about that.

Most teachers in schools where I was assigned worked at two or three jobs, and taught private lessons as well. Everyone has to find a way to make a living, and does whatever he has to do in order to survive.

I do not know how the present system is working, but I am reasonably sure that there are still "loopholes" and that creative people are still finding ways to be paid for work that they never do. Another tribute to the genius of Cairenes!

Returning to the Mugamma, it is a place that has seen some violent clashes in the past, and anyone who isn't strong enough might be broken on its lethargy alone. The office workers find creative ways to fill their time. Telephones work well there, and much time is spent talking on them. Carefully tended gardens flourish on balconies and inside windows where the morning sun floods in. All manner of extraneous work is done, for extra money, and paperwork for a single department can be completed more speedily with enough *baksheesh*. The problems come when the work is taken to the next department that has to deal with it. More baksheesh is paid per department until the cost is prohibitive unless the paperwork is vital. Lots of people stop short of completion.

Passports, licenses of various kinds, registrations, birth and marriage certificates and more are the province of The Mugamma, but it has failed in its purpose of "togetherness" altogether.

....

There are few things that are not found in Cairo, but there are many things that are found only there. The beauties of the ancient world, of course; Sakkara and the Giza Pyramids, have stood far longer than almost any other manmade thing, but the clever mix of all things that comprise Cairo today is a great tapestry that has taken centuries, even millenia, to blend together, and will continue to enlarge as long as the city lives. That, to me, is the great genius of Cairo, and the thing that draws me back to the city even in the midst of a very comfortable life in Oregon. Cairo actually exists, in all of its incarnations, as much as the fabled but faded city of Timbuktu, but Cairo is still dynamically and dramatically alive, and readily accessible.

Above all else, Cairo *is*, and that is all that is finally important.

Religion

*I*SLAM AND CHRISTIANITY—CHRISTIANITY AND Islam. Only two religions are permitted for the citizens of Egypt. There are some
similarities between the two religions, and many obvious differences,
but there are subtle differences as well.

The indigenous Christian Church in Egypt is known as the Coptic
Orthodox Church. It is not a part of any other Orthodox or Catholic
church, but separate, except for many similar doctrines. The Coptic
Church is an ancient church, founded by St. Mark—who wrote the
gospel—and has been greatly influential in early decisions that developed the Christian religion, including the council at Nicea where
the well known Creed was adopted. There are several Coptic mon-
asteries in Egypt, and even today there are new members who take
vows there. From the third century, monks have lived in the Egyptian
desert in isolation and privation, trying to find their way to God in
that place.

Coptic churches today are filled with people on the high holy
days; Christmas, which they celebrate on January 6, and Easter. I attended a Christmas Eve service with a Christian teacher in Cairo, and
the church was overflowing into the front courtyard so that we could
hardly get in through the gate. There are several Coptic churches in

Cairo, and a large cathedral (which looks something like an athletic field house) as well. The cathedral is one of the last religious buildings the Coptic Church has been allowed to build. Egyptian Christians are proud of their heritage, although they are fairly quiet about it among the many Muslims who are their neighbors.

Christians are encouraged to convert to Islam, but Muslims cannot convert to Christianity. There are no arguments allowed about this. Muslims, the name for followers of Islam, believe that they possess the pure, final religion, sent by God into the world, and that the entire world will one day be Muslim. Some Muslims believe that violent confrontation with infidels—anyone who is not Muslim—is encouraged, even demanded by God in their holy book, the Koran. For those who hold this belief, their actions are frequently predicated upon it, as well as their desire to hurry worldwide conversion along.

An interesting phenomenon is that Muslim women who have difficulty conceiving a child sometimes go to the Christian Church in their village or city to pray to Mary, the mother of Jesus. Muslims believe that Jesus was a great prophet, although he was superseded by the greatest prophet, Muhammed.

No other religions are allowed for Egyptians. There are followers of other religions living in the land, but they are not Egyptian, and there are no temples, churches, or buildings for worship for these religions in Egypt, as there are no functioning synagogues allowed now. (The ancient synagogue in Old Cairo is a museum,)

In parts of the countryside, Christians and Muslims live well together as neighbors and even friends, but in other places, animosity separates them, and whichever is in the minority in that village (usually Christians) lives in a constant state of tension.

The government of Egypt declares that there is a small (four to six percent) group of Christians in the population, but some observers think the percentage is larger, perhaps ten to fifteen percent. The law states that you are whatever religion you are born into.

No census has been taken to determine exactly how many Christians or Muslims there are in the country.

Within the last few decades the government has taken more steps to repress Christians in some ways, although they are still represented in the government itself and some are among the wealthier class of Egyptians. The government has placed a moratorium on new church buildings, and has also condemned and destroyed (in the name of public works) a few church buildings. Some of these have been relocated, but others have not.

A more subtle point is that no one is allowed to have no stated religion, or to be atheist. Every Egyptian must be, officially at least, Muslim or Christian. There is no freedom of choice in the matter. People who have come to Egypt from countries where religion is *entirely* a choice find this concept hard to accept. Not that anyone born outside of Egypt, or of Egyptian parentage, could be Egyptian—naturalization is not available—but the *idea* of such governmental control of religion is difficult to understand.

The concept of monotheism is not unique to Judaism, Christianity, or Islam. Over 3500 years ago, the Pharaoh Akhenatun, father of Tutankhamun, came to believe in only one god, the Aten, who had a symbolic, disc- like appearance, unlike any other ancient Egyptian god. Followers believed he acted alone in creation. Judaism was also founded on monotheism, and Christianity, as an offshoot of Judaism, believes the same thing, although Muslims accuse Christians of worshipping three gods rather than one. A great pillar of the Muslim faith is that there is but one God, Allah, and that Muhammed is his prophet. (Allah is pronounced Al—LAH, the stress being on the last syllable.) According to Muslims, Christians worship The Father, The Son, and The Holy Spirit, three Gods, but Christians maintain that their God is a three-in-one God, and that there is equality within the One God. That is a great pillar of Christianity, and is considered the mystery of the Holy Trinity. Sometimes it all becomes rather confusing.

Egyptians are usually identified within their own country by their religion. Faith is the most important component of life there, and the struggle to maintain faith, whether of the dominant or other kind, is the most important of life's struggles. I have seen people express their feelings about religion in various ways, but never dispassionately. After many conversations and much observation and thought, I believe that because Arabs as a whole were so very poor for so long has a role in the current revitalization of Islam. To me it seems that Arabs believe that the development of oil in their lands is a unique blessing from Allah, and that they are now, because of such great wealth, obligated to bring the rest of the world to Allah through Islam. Religion aside, it is also very likely that they feel that the world has ignored them, and that oil money should give them a greater resource for prestige and power on the world stage. That is their due.

Another of the basic pillars of Islam is prayer, and Muslims have prayers five times each day, beginning a half hour before dawn and ending a half hour after sunset. The muezzin, who is now broadcast from minarets through high volume electronic speakers, calls the people to prayer at those times. In Cairo, called " the city of a thousand minarets," the call to prayer first sounds like a vast number of mosquitoes in the distance, coming rapidly closer, until the moment when a nearby mosque begins the call, and for many non-Muslims the hope of sleep in the early morning is shattered. I learned to live with that, despite the fact that my flat was directly across the street from a mosque.

Egypt seems to be becoming more devoutly Muslim. This is most apparent to an observer in the style of dress women use. Fifty years ago women were freed from the *burka*—covering—and were allowed to be in public with no head covering or outer robe, as long as they wore modest clothing and did not accentuate their bodies.

At present most young women prefer to wear head coverings and very modest clothing with long sleeves, necklines just under their chins, and nearly ankle length skirts. This could be the choice of a father or husband, but often this is a response of women who want to show that they are God-fearing and want to be a good example for their children and especially for their husbands. Some of the older women, who were part of the movement to discard these coverings, do not wear them even today, when the mood of the country is more conservative and their faithful observance of religion may be called into question. One young man I know did not really want his wife to wear headscarves and the very modest dress, but agreed that she could if she felt that they were necessary, which she did. She wore the coverings sweetly and modestly and is one of the finest people I have known in Cairo.

Sometimes things work another way. I know a young girl at a school who cried for days because her father forced her to begin to cover. She had no desire to wear the head covering, especially, and had that forced upon her by a father who wanted to see that she "fit in" so she could get a good husband when the time came.

Other young women told me that they were glad to wear the modest homemade clothes. By wearing them on a daily basis they saved enough money to buy some of the beautiful evening dresses that they longed to wear, and on some Friday nights (after the religious observations were over), they attend parties in the very best hotels wearing those lovely things, makeup artfully applied, headscarves forgotten.

Another story has an element of humor, although the underlying conditions are hardly funny. I noticed a completely covered woman bringing her young children to school day after day. By "completely" I mean a veil over her face and gloves on her hands, as well as a very large burka that dropped to her well dressed feet. This kind of garb was unusual for Cairo, and I asked a friend about it. "Do you see that old man walking ahead of her?" he asked. I saw an old man about a half block up the street, a man of large girth and a scraggly long beard. "That's her husband," he said. "She was forced to marry him because he's rich. She is young and beautiful, everyone says, but she covers herself completely to hide her embarrassment." Apparently the husband thought that she was a dutiful wife, walking respectfully far behind him, and was proud of himself. "The reason she walks so far back," my friend said, "is that she doesn't want anyone to know that he is her husband."

"Islam" is an Arabic word that means "submission," and "Muslim" is "one who submits." Muslims believe that the Koran was written by the finger of God, and that part of it was given, by the angel Gabriel, to the prophet Muhammed when he was taken into heaven from Jerusalem. The Koran is, therefore, as central to their religion as Jesus is to Christianity.

During Ramadan, there is a night when Muslims celebrate the giving of the Koran, and the mosques are full of people at prayer. Women seem to be encouraged to attend prayers on that night, and there is a chant that is sung by both the men and women; the loveliest thing I ever heard coming from a mosque. It is sung in close harmony and repeated many times, and will always live in my memory.

Ramadan is an entire month that is set aside for religious observation. The month is not stationary, but moves backward through the year, following the cycle of the moon. Noted by most of the world as a month of fasting, Muslims do fast all day during Ramadan, neither eating nor drinking anything. But just at sunset, the fast is broken with a small meal. Then, as the night progresses, the fasting turns to feasting, and extended families visit each other for elaborate meals and lots of visiting, gossip, and fun. Children are given presents, and everyone has a congenial and joyful night. Many people stay up all night, and sleep during the day, although some try to work at their regular jobs, going in later and leaving earlier as the month wears on. Everyone accommodates Ramadan. There is little choice in the matter.

Not only are food, drink, and sexual relations prohibited during the fast of Ramadan, but also smoking. That is what causes a lot of men to break into nicotine fits then. I was in a taxi one afternoon near the end of Ramadan, and the driver came upon a blocked road; too many cars that were trying to get through a narrow space. Everyone was honking and screaming at everyone else. Tempers were fragile at best. Finally, my driver leaped out of the car, taking his ignition key with him, climbed onto the hood just in front of the windshield and sat there glowering. Other drivers jumped out of their taxis and ran toward him, but he sat firmly, yelling something at the others. Horns were honking and people were shouting all around, and I thought a fight might begin. I laid my taxi fare on the seat and got out. I headed around the small midan and crossed a street to get close to the building where I lived.

As I turned away and walked around the corner I could hear the noise of people and car horns. I turned into the entrance to my building and didn't look back until I had gotten into my own apartment, opened the curtains and looked down at the Midan. The taxi and driver were still there, the shouting more subdued by the distance, but soon, I knew, all would be filled with Ramadan peace. It would take a few drinks of water and some tobacco, but good will would be restored.

Perhaps my best memory of Ramadan was on a night very early in the month, when I returned to Cairo after a trip to the U. S. I noticed, as I claimed a taxi and started toward the city, that there was not the usual clamor inside the airport, and that the road leading into the city was quieter. Then I remembered that it was Ramadan, and that the sun had set as I arrived. The people were enjoying *Iftar*, the breakfast that follows the day of fasting. All the city was lighted, and the air seemed fresh and clean as we rode along. We came to a mosque beside the highway. The gates were closed, but they were hung with lighted lamps which cast a glow all around, and there was almost no sound at that moment. It was a quiet and reflective time, and I knew that all the Muslims, wherever in the city they might be, had stopped along the street—where long tables of food had been spread out under the trees for all to partake—or were in their houses, beginning a night of visiting and feasting. It was Ramadan, at the time for Iftar, and the world was right again, and everyone was happy.

Streets, Sidewalks, and Stairs

I ARRIVED IN CAIRO ON a Thursday evening in early September just as the sun was setting. The trip from San Francisco was long, and I had little sleep until after I boarded a nearly empty jumbo jet in Rome and could lie across a middle section row and sleep most of the way to Cairo.

It was the first time I had traveled there, the first time I had crossed the Atlantic, and the first time I was ever so far from home. I felt seriously lonely and fought off a bout of homesickness, but when I woke up from the nap and looked out the window all of that left me. We were passing over the delta of the Nile, which was lushly green just below, but to the right, the sand spread out in a long tawny line toward the great Sahara. The color was not at all grey, but looked like some sort of African beast-color that a lion might wear. The desert land was featureless and desolate, but I loved the fact that there was such a huge unpopulated place in the midst of the world as I knew it. I watched and waited for the first glimpses of Cairo.

After a while, I finally saw some buildings, then more, and the plane began to descend. From the air the city looked as tawny as the desert, for we had left the Delta behind, and despite the fact that the buildings were tall, the city had an overall appearance of sand and dust. How different everything is on the ground!

Cairo is an oasis. It has a lot of green—trees and gardens and midans of various sizes throughout the city. There are also many gardens that cannot be seen from the streets, with beautiful bougainvillea and other vining plants spread across the tops of walls and over gates. The Nile flows through what seems the center of the city, with two prominent islands mid-water. At one point the Nile is so wide between the islands that the shore on either side is almost a mile from the center of the river.

Cairo is narrow by modern city standards, fitting tightly between the western plateau where the pyramids stand and the Mukattam Hills on the east. The city is somewhat longer, north to south, but doesn't seem nearly large enough to hold the millions of people who throng there day and night. It is the largest city in Africa and one of the largest in the world.

At the airport I found a car waiting for me, with one of the administrators waiting as well. In a very short time we were on our way into the city, having in some way cut through the checks at the gate. Those very gates are known to some travelers as "The Gates Of Hell" because they are so frustrating to negotiate. Fortunately, I missed all that. We drove into Cairo along a highway that looked a lot like a freeway, then into the heart of the city and out again until we finally arrived at a hotel in Zamalek where I would live for the next few weeks.

Zamalek is one of the islands in the Nile. It was the British area during their time in Egypt, and in some places large villas stood back from the street; the houses for the British when they were there. The villas are now divided into apartments, and some have become schools or offices for Egyptians, or residences for foreign embassies. Many of the gardens remain. I saw some of them later that night. I couldn't sleep at all and felt a sense of apprehension so I got up and walked between two and four a.m. Going out in the late night didn't seem dangerous, and wasn't, but I had no way of knowing that at the time. I went into the street in front of the hotel entrance and walked as far down as I could, keeping the light from the hotel's distant illumination as a guide.

Finally, after the walk, I settled into my room and began to read from a guidebook I had received at the airport. I found that there was an Anglican Cathedral in Zamalek that didn't look too far away by the map. I fell asleep after deciding to go there for the Friday morning service the next day.

I am Episcopalian, a part of the Anglican Communion, and finding the cathedral so close gave me some comfort. I knew that the church used the same liturgy worldwide, and that I would find a service I knew and loved and understood in that place.

I didn't sleep long, so taking the map in my pocket, began the long walk across Zamalek to All Saint's Cathedral, on Sharia Michel Lutfallah. I knew that I was stepping into a new world, but had no idea how great an influence those streets, and especially the cathedral, would have over me in the years that I lived in Cairo.

I walked toward the river, about half a block away, and turned left at the Pizza Hut that stood on a prominent corner near the hotel. That Pizza Hut was only one of many in the city. There were also other American fast food places, and McDonald's came in with a flourish, opening several restaurants at the same time about a year after I went to Cairo.

From the Pizza Hut I turned down Sharia Abu Al Feda for a distance, following the Nile, with pleasant river views on my right. I soon came to the street that led to the cathedral, Sharia Sitta Wa Ishrin Yulyu.

The street had a peculiar look on the map, a wide gray path cutting diagonally across the island, with heavy black lines on either side. I understood when I saw it. The whole thing was a flyover with a double street, one above and one below. It extended all the way across the island, and for those who wanted to cross quickly, the upper level was as close to a freeway as I ever found in Egypt. After I moved to Dokki I traveled across the flyover several times a week, getting off at the only exit at the far eastern edge of Zamalek.

Shopkeepers were just opening for the day as I walked onto the street. They were sweeping sidewalks in front of their shops, using short handled brooms with long curved straws attached, looking something like the scimitar blades of ancient knives. Most of them were wearing traditional *gallabeyas,* a long sleeved open shirt that reached the ground, and they tended to be the same tawny color as the desert around the bottom hem. They were further stained with what looked like coffee or tobacco, or both. The men also wore small, often dirty, caps or turbans on their heads, and some sort of heavy sandals on their feet. Although a lot of men wear western style jeans or suits, the gallabeya is the standard wear for men, and is seen in every part of the city, worn by all classes of people. Most women in Cairo favor modest clothing, including headscarves. Gallabeyas worn by the felahin women are often very colorful, bright with yellows and greens or blues. Women do not tend to wear jewelry or any adornment except earrings.

Sitta Wa Ishrin Yulyu is lined with shops, from one end to the other, most with large plate glass windows facing the street. I saw lots of shoe stores, filled with shiny metal shelves and mirrors and chandeliers, some cafes, which were already busy at the time I went past, and produce markets displaying beautiful bright red tomatoes common to Egypt; the most flavorful I have ever eaten. There were also unusually shaped carrots, about four inches wide across the top, tapering quickly to a point; about four inches long as well. Diamond shaped Egyptian carrots.

There were lots of other vegetables on display in boxes along the street, but many were seriously wilted and would need a long soaking bath in ice water to revive. They also sold eggs, which could be bought in any quantity, placed in plastic and packed along with vegetables into large bags. I could never get them home without a few breaking. Eggs were priced individually; you could buy a dozen, but that wasn't the standard package in Cairo.

The eggs were not clean, either. They had chicken manure clinging to them and the manure was filled with feathers and straw. I had to take them home and wash them in soapy bleach water before storing them in the refrigerator. That had to be done quickly. I ate a lot of eggs in Cairo because I didn't want to buy meat unless I was eating at a reliable restaurant. The problem with meat was that I saw the butcher shops that morning on Sitta Wa Ishrin Yulyu.

Butchers hang their products out over the street on large hooks, and people passing can brush against them, sit beneath and smoke, or lean against a carcass as they talk. These large carcasses are often covered with insects, and they seem alive as the flies buzz around them. A butcher would come outside, cut a portion from a carcass, weigh and wrap it and send it off with a smiling, satisfied customer. The flies then resettled along the fresh cut, and everybody had a feast.

I didn't go inside the butcher shops, but the meat hung outside was enough to dissuade me from buying. There were several butchers the length of the street, and some were even less appealing than others. I generally rejected local meat from then on, although I'm not usually squeamish about food. The treatment of meat was just too much for my western sensitivities to accept.

There were antique stores on and near the street, mostly on small side streets that seemed broad and clean. They were filled with a mix of things, some of them beautiful and seriously valuable. I didn't ever buy anything there except for a great looking old ring for my wife.

As I walked along I looked ahead and noticed that the street soon came to an end against a barrier that contained a small opening to a pedestrian bridge across the Nile. I started looking for a street that ran toward Sitta Wa Ishrin Yulyu, so that I could go on over to find the cathedral. As I looked down at the next corner I found a sign above a gate a block away—"All Saint's Cathedral." I had arrived.

The cathedral compound was empty. Not one person was in sight. I stepped through the gate and found a long concrete courtyard in front of the cathedral, a small street for parking in front of that, and another paved courtyard in front of the British School that faced the cathedral church.

The cathedral itself was a spare contemporary building, made of tawny cement with large fluted front walls rising to diamond shapes under a roof that ascended to a lotus-petal-shaped tower in the center. It was not particularly beautiful, but seemed more exotic than most of the buildings I had seen that morning. I went up to sit on the long front porch on the north side, waiting for someone to come to open the doors.

After a long wait, I had just decided that I had made a mistake and was ready to leave when the gate opened and a young woman entered. She was Sudanese, she told me, and had arrived in Cairo just a few days before. We chatted and waited together and wondered if we had the right day. Finally, the gate opened again, just before eleven, and a priest entered.

He greeted us and knocked on the front door of the church. A little later we heard a scraping sound, and an invisible person opened the door to let us in. The place was dark and cool inside, and we talked with the priest as he prepared for the Friday morning service. The time had been changed from ten to eleven, he told us, and led us to the side chapel where the congregation would meet.

At the conclusion of the service, the priest mentioned that he was in need of a pianist for the Friday morning Eucharist. I had been in church music all my life, since I was sixteen, and told him that I was available. His face told me that he was skeptical, but he said that he'd like to have me play, on a trial basis, the next Friday. I did, and was the pianist there until I left Cairo. He later asked me to serve on the cathedral council; I was doubtful, but he assured me that all would work out, and it did. I spent a lot of time with the council, working on various problems and programs for the cathedral church, and that was a great thing for me. It filled the empty places when I was very new, and provided contacts that I would never have had otherwise.

....

In the evenings when I sat looking out my reception room windows at my house in Dokki, I could see parts of the city clearly. Egyptians love neon lights, bright lights, any kind of lights, and I could see the tall buildings near downtown, the Radio building with the blinking red lights on the antenna at the top, the Ramses Hilton, and the Cairo Tower, all glowing amid the diffused lights of the city. Although I couldn't see the Nile because of all the buildings crowded up against it, I could see across to the other side. Directly to the east was the Nile Hilton Hotel. My view was of the top floors and the large sign that proclaimed the title in English and Arabic. I knew that the Cairo Museum was behind on the left, and that Tahrir Square, the center of Cairo, lay in front of the museum. The Mugamma was dark at night and not easily visible, but it was there, across the square, as was the American University, hidden away behind the others.

On the Dokki side of the Nile I could see the Ibn Sina hospital, a very tall building just across Midan Tehran and about a block from my house. I couldn't see much of Sharai Mussadaq, the street that ran in front of the hospital, or the corner where I generally found a taxi. I could glimpse parts of them between buildings, but the most prominent feature close to my house was the Sharia Dokki flyover, a raised portion of the street that ran from north to south through Dokki, the area in Giza that had become home.

A flyover is a raised street. Sometimes the original street runs beneath it, or sometimes just the cross streets pass under the structure, with shops or parking facilities under the parts between the cross streets. Sharia Sitta Wa Ishrin Yulyu (26th July Street) is an example of the former, and Sharia Dokki of the latter.

The Dokki Flyover was always full of cars, and I could hear them faintly if I opened a window. I was fortunate, everyone who visited told me, that I lived in a quiet area of the city. That was true except for five times a day when the call to prayer was broadcast forcefully from the mosque on the street behind. Then I couldn't hear anything else. The call to prayer was an important daily event, heeded by the faithful, and could probably be heard by even those who were mostly deaf. I did, however, learn to sleep through the earliest call, a half hour before dawn every morning.

The Dokki Flyover was built on huge cement pillars, and of the several streets crossing under it, the largest was Sharia Tahrir, which continued downtown to Tahrir Square. Although many streets in Cairo are small and some are even winding, the large streets or boulevards are straight and very wide. Their width was a great foresight, a gift to the future by street planners over one hundred years ago. Sharia Tahrir is an example of the very widest of boulevards.

The French and the British designed streets according to some plan that was laid out long ago. They were deep with high curbs on either side, and were crowned (higher) in the center and lowered at the far edges. The high curbs were about two and a half feet above the street level. This was, in the old days, the sewer system for the city, and it flowed along toward the Nile, pulled by gravity. In the 1950's a modern sewer was excavated under the streets and put to work in Cairo. I can well imagine the difference that made! Some parts of Cairo today, especially in the Mukkotam hills, still have open sewers flowing, but that is the exception now.

Midans are very popular in the city. They are the round-abouts that the British use, and are supposed to offer drivers easy entrances and exits. More often, they confound the problems, and cars, taxis, and sometimes even buses cross from the center to the outer edge abruptly, causing everyone else to stop, and many fender-bender accidents. Nothing is ever smoothly or easily accomplished when driving in Cairo.Every kind of conveyance travels on Cairo's streets. Cars, buses, a few bicycles, donkey carts, motor bikes, rickshaw-like vehicles, pedestrians and herds of animals all find their way across the city through major and secondary streets. Many of the wagons, carts, and rickshaws are heavily ornamented in order to attract attention to whatever the occupant is selling. Bright blues and reds, yellows and greens are the favorites, with garish patterns and symbols covering the entire vehicle.

There are streets that resemble freeways, but there are no real freeways because there are no limited access roads. Everything that moves on the streets is allowed to go anywhere on any street or highway. That is a danger, of course, but to the Egyptian that is their right and if they choose to endanger themselves (or others) that is their right as well.

I have no love for Cairo's city buses, and very rarely rode on them, and then only when I was with an Egyptian. It was impossible for me to ride most buses, anyway. I watched the buses arrive and depart from their stops and knew that I could never get on or off one. To board a bus at a stop, not a major station, the rider had to run up while it was still moving and, at the same time, depositing other passengers at the stop. He had to grab a hand extended from the bus door which would pull him up and into the bus. There were always many extended hands, a tribute to the camaraderie of bus passengers.

In the other case, departing passengers would leap from the bus steps and run about ten feet in the direction of the moving bus so that they could retain balance and not topple. That was a successful operation whenever I saw it, but I'm sure that there were incidents of falling and worse.

When I had to ride the bus, I boarded while it was sitting at a station and got off at another station. I knew I could never leap on or off.

For obvious reasons, women did not board or leave moving buses. They got on and off at stations. There may be buses for women only, as there are women's cars on the Metro, but I didn't ever see one.

I did ride the Metro often. It was built by the French in the mid to late 1980's, and is still a wonder to ride. It is efficient and fairly clean, with convenient stops up and down the line. The first line went from northeast to south, El Marg to Helwan, and the second line, opened in 2000, goes in a north to southwest direction, from Shobra to El Mounib in Giza, after passing over the Nile

Metro trains are always full to absolutely packed. Once I had to stand the whole distance from the Tahrir station to Maadi, a suburb some miles south of the city center, while squeezed by a mob of people. I had gotten on the train with some new acquaintances from the U.K., but we couldn't quite stay together so we traveled all the way within arms length but couldn't talk at all. When we got to the station I shouted that we had arrived, and the three of us pushed our way out the door. Gridlock is all too common on the Metro.

Passenger trains that travel to the north or south of Egypt are available, but most are unpleasant and dirty, filled with smoke (from cigarettes and cigars,) and slow. One exception is the fast-train from Cairo to Alexandria, on the shore of the Mediterranean Sea, the northern boundary of Egypt.

The fast-train was built by the French not long before they built the Metro, and is as sophisticated as the fast-trains in France. This train is non-smoking, although many of the men who ride it try to smoke, and takes about an hour and a half to get to the destination. There are two or three choices for class level, with first class a bit tonier and more expensive. All classes seem rather luxurious, however. I was traveling on the fast-train with friends who had their baby with them when an Egyptian man started smoking. I asked him to stop. He ignored me, so I spoke carefully in Arabic. He jumped up and berated me in English while he left the car, only to stand in the short passage between cars and smoke.

Cairo buses are notorious for many reasons, but dangerous driving is probably the biggest problem in the system. I have seen buses careen through intersections, bump into supports under flyovers, nearly topple from cornering too fast, and generally create fear and a lot of consternation. My favorite bus story is one that includes a couple of taxis and their truly intrepid drivers.

One morning I set out to go to a school far out on Sharia Al Haram, the Pyramids Road. I lived in Dokki, Giza, not too far from the east end of Al Haram , and was headed north when the taxi had to stop for a traffic policeman and was soundly rear-ended by a bus. The policemen kept on directing traffic, but as the taxi driver got out to look at the damage, the bus roared around him and was gone. The policeman waved it through and the bus went sliding down the street as though it were trying to make up time. Although keeping to a time schedule is never a serious consideration for Egyptian buses, I have observed.

Later that day, after I left the school, I got another taxi on Al Haram and was headed home. We came near the place of the morning accident when we were stopped by another policeman and were hit in the rear by another bus. This time the jolt wasn't as heavy, so the driver didn't try to look at the damage right away, but drove on down the street shaking his head.

Taxis are plentiful in all of Cairo, and I could find one driving along looking for fares at any hour of the day or night. Not all taxis are the same, however. I have been in some that were choked with fumes, and others have had mechanical breakdowns while I was traveling in them. They are hard working vehicles, and are not always kept up so far as cleanliness and-or mechanics are concerned. Few are air conditioned, and can be terribly hot almost any time of the year. They are safer than buses, but present their own kind of danger.

One evening just at dusk I was with an Egyptian friend riding in a taxi near the Pyramids Road—Sharia Al Haram—when a bicyclist darted across in front. The driver hit him, and the boy went flying. The street was narrow, hardly wide enough for two cars to pass, with houses forming walls on either side. They were really large apartment blocks that were several stories tall, filled with families; they were newer, but of cheap construction.

As soon as the boy on the bike fell against the wall of a house on the right side of the street, a crowd began to develop, and some women began wailing. I didn't think the boy had been killed, but was concerned about him. The taxi driver, on the other hand, was concerned about his passengers as well as his own skin. The car had hardly stopped when the driver got out. I thought he was going to find out about the condition of the boy, but he moved the bike, which lay in our way, jumped back into the taxi, and drove away as fast as he could.

I realized then that I had been in danger just as much as the driver. Crowds of felahin sometimes act as a mob without thought. The boy had been hit by the taxi, and, therefore, according to their reasoning, anyone involved with the taxi was guilty of hitting the boy and could bring rapid retribution to anyone they might think responsible. The driver, aware of that kind of reasoning, got away as fast as he could.

There was no question of blame. The boy had turned across too late, and he must have known that the taxi would hit him. He had to face the consequences of his action, whatever they would be, and the crowd didn't have time to become a mob. It was over and we were gone before anyone had time to react, and I never heard anything about it again.

That taxi ride was an unusual adventure for another reason as well. We were headed to Imbaba, a section of Cairo where I had never been. I was told, by the administrators of the program I worked for, that it was full of extremists and that no one should go there. The young man I was with was an English teacher who taught a class in a Coptic church in Imbaba, and had persuaded me to go with him to the class that night, assuring me that all would be well. I thought everything would be fine after the incident with the boy on the bicycle, and settled into the long ride across the city.

Having never been to Imbaba I asked no questions as we left the taxi and started to walk, but after many blocks and a fast pace I wondered aloud why we couldn't have gone further in the taxi.

"Oh, the taxi wouldn't take us any further," Shady told me. "Taxis won't go into Imbaba. The people from the mosques shoot at them sometimes."

I considered for a moment. "But why do they shoot at them?"

"Because they carry western passengers and the men here hate the west."

We got out of Imbaba alive and I never saw it again, except to look at it across the river from Zamalek and wonder how I ever had allowed myself to be taken there.

....

There are a few true sidewalks in Cairo; most are downtown. In residential areas the streets serve for walking as well as riding in whatever conveyances are available. Things are different in various parts of the city, of course.

Most of the business buildings and stores outside of the downtown area have a setback from the street that looks like a sidewalk. It is, in a way, but is also different. The "sidewalk" serves only that building. These sidewalks are independent things, and are dangerous for someone who doesn't know how to use them. They are not meant to be connected to each other, and may vary in height between buildings from less than an inch to several feet. In some places they are connected with small ramps made of asphalt, or by a stair, to provide easier access from one building to the next. In other places they simply end at the edge of one building, and begin anew on an entirely different level in front of the next. The other level may be higher, lower, or nearly even, but is usually dangerously different.

I apply three "rules" for walking in Cairo. 1.) Don't walk at night without a light. 2.) Always step into the street (where it is generally level), walk to the next building you are going to, and step up from the street. 3.) Keep your eyes on the ground at all times wherever you walk, inside or outside. You never know.

The last rule applies because there are many large openings, sometimes innocently covered, sometimes wide open, in the areas near the entrance doors to a building. These "holes" are used for the water main shutoff, sewer access (which is normally covered), and sometimes for other utilities. I have seen them more than a foot deep, standing open near a doorway. At times, people step on what we call man-hole covers, only to have the cover slip or break and send one foot down into the hole, which is often the sewer access for that building. That is not pleasant at all. They can cause injury, but certainly a noxious clean up.

I saw a young student, a girl of about fifteen, step on a cover that was at the bottom of a short flight of stairs. The cover tilted, and her foot and leg got caught in the sewer access box halfway up to her knee. Some of her friends extricated her, and she left crying. She must have been hurt, but the humiliation would have been greater. I learned never to step on those covers, and I still avoid them wherever I am.

Watching your step is a good rule inside as well as outside. One day I was crossing the lobby of a hotel where I was waiting to meet a friend. We were going to have dinner in the restaurant there. The lobby was large, with brown and tan marble floor and walls. Everything was unified, and the shiny marble created the feeling of a seamless room. But it wasn't. A single step, for whatever reason, extended the full length of the lobby near the western side of the room, close to the entrance to the restaurant. While I was walking across, I failed to "keep my eye on the floor" and stepped off that single step, stumbled wildly a couple of times, and hit the wall with a hard thud. I'm glad the wall was there, or I would have landed spread out on the floor.

As far as I know, we must have enjoyed the dinner that followed, but have never been sure. My memory seems to have stopped against that wall.

In much of the world—I had never thought it wasn't all of the world—stairs are of even height, that is, each step is the same distance above the next, and that makes them fairly easy to use. This is not the case in Cairo.

Although some of the buildings do have even stairs, many don't.

I lived in what had to be considered one of the best new buildings in the area, and the stairs there were uneven, especially at the bottom or the top of each flight. When I had to walk down in the dark, I measured and counted the steps on each floor, found that some had one less or one more step, and that often one of the steps in a flight was shorter or higher than the others. This made everything seem a little off balance, especially in the dark, because I could never remember exactly where the differences were, and had to grope slowly along to find them each time. Fifteen flights are a lot of steps to remember.

Several of my Egyptian friends lived in apartments or flats in Giza, near Sharia Al Haram. These buildings were usually five story affairs with two flats on each floor. The stairwells were often dark, with burned out (or appropriated) lightbulbs, and the passages held garbage bins or whatever refuse the families wanted the garbage collectors to take. They also held unusual stairways.

There are hundreds, multiple hundreds, of these buildings, and they all had gone up within about a decade. I am not sure if they were government construction, or private, but they were low cost and were affordable to the people who couldn't afford much else. They were lined along streets and wide boulevards that were surfaced with unpaved sand, and sometimes ground water seeped into the streets creating large wet sand pits where cars and carts got stuck. The flats weren't the best, but were certainly not the worst. They did have plumbing and bathrooms and electricity. Rooms were small, but families were used to living in small spaces. There was no glass in the windows, only wooden shutters—another thing common to most houses in Cairo. Sometimes enterprising owners who could afford glass put it in, but that wasn't much protection from mosquitoes, the chief purpose of glass in Cairo because there is virtually no rain.

The stairs, however, were a series of open concrete boxes that ascended from floor to floor. The boxes were built empty, but when filled with the readily available sand, they became a soft set of steps to climb. When part of the sand was kicked out and had not been replenished, the steps became very uneven and were hard to use.

One of the families I knew who lived in one of those places had a lovely flat on the top floor of a building. It was clean and newly painted, furnished with lots of books and an interesting mix of things, and the dining table was always laid with their very best linen and china. The food was a feast as well, and the flat was as wholesome and homey as anywhere I have ever gone for dinner.

$\mathcal{P}laces$

$\mathcal{M}$Y HOUSE IN CAIRO was large, filled with light from window walls along the north and west of the flat that were covered with filmy curtains. It was on the fifteenth floor of a twenty story building, which I called my "fifteenth floor walk-up"—when the electricity was off I had to walk all the way. I got used to that. The house was probably the biggest place I have ever lived, nearly three thousand square feet, and most of the time I was there alone. It had an entry area, a dining area, and a large reception room (Middle Eastern for living room) that was open to the rest. It was one space but had been cleverly divided with furniture and small alcoves on the sides, and could handle a large party with no problem at all.

The room had been decorated by someone who studied design in France, the owner told me, and was beautiful—filled with antiques, new sofas and chairs, old carpets, and some huge floor pillows and accent tables. The flat was furnished, which in Cairo means that *everything* necessary for living there was included. I had all the pots and pans and dishes I needed in the kitchen, towels and bedsheets and anything else required to set up housekeeping. There was even a set of "good" china in the buffet in the dining room, and a credenza in the entry held tablecloths and napkins for more formal use. I may have used them once. It was an expensive flat, but the company I worked for provided housing. I had only to find the right place and move in.

It is the custom in Egypt for rents to be paid in advance—six month or one year allotments—so I had to be sure that I found the right flat. All the terms need to be negotiated before the papers are signed, and the terms must be strictly observed by the tenant. The owner of a flat can be less punctilious, so anything could happen if the owner took a dislike to the tenant. I was always glad that I was dealing with a woman of integrity in matters concerning my flat, although I had to arrange things with her brother at our first meeting because she was a widow. It would not have been proper for her to negotiate the terms of the contract alone; she had to rely on a male family member who was considered to be responsible for her.

I found the flat after about three weeks in a hotel, with the help of a rental agent who managed to get me to it in record time one afternoon, so that no one else would get ahead of me. I was grateful for her help, but had some misgivings when she drove down the pedestrian walk on the Nile bridge and swerved carelessly through the traffic, never heeding red lights or much else as we catapulted through Cairo and Giza to get to my new house in less than thirty minutes. I was never taken for such a ride again, and I rode with a lot of taxi drivers.

I had three large bedrooms, including a master suite with bath—with a refrigerator in the room, a long hallway along the bedroom wing, and two great bathrooms that were completely lined with ceramic tile. The largest bath included an automatic washer. I had an outside clothesline that extended from a window, but preferred to dry my clothes in closets because they got dirty if I hung them outside. The kitchen was small, but was completely tiled, and the place was palatial as far as I was concerned. The floor plan is best described as a railroad flat, but that doesn't do justice to its beauty and comfort.

There were electric wall heaters in the reception room and dining area, but I never used them. It was rarely cold enough. I used the air conditioners most of the time. There was no central air, but each room had its own unit, and there were four in the reception room. Cairo is a very hot place.

The house came with a maid who was in once a week and cleaned everything, even any dishes I had left in the sink. She polished the wood floors and washed the tiled ones, cleaned all the furniture and even washed the curtains a couple of times. She offered to do my laundry, but I declined, thinking I should at least do that much for myself. Friends persuaded me to hire a *maquagee*, an ironing man, who came to my house every week and ironed whatever pieces I gave him. Their argument was that people needed to have jobs and some income, and that I could provide that for at least two; the maid and the maquagee. I paid both every time they came. (I had to leave the money on the credenza for the maid, who had a key to get in. I could not be at home while she was there. Propriety would not allow a man and woman to be behind closed doors without supervision.) The cost was small for the services they performed, and I had an easy life in Cairo so far as house work was concerned.

My house was a refuge and a haven of quiet. I could listen to my shortwave radio and find wonderful music, read books, or just look out at the world as I sat on the sofa at the end of the reception room, surrounded by huge windows.

....

I often walked home from the school where I worked that was nearest my house. I lived about a mile from that school, and I walked home—rather than to school in the morning—because I wanted to arrive fresh and clean. On the way home I liked to walk along a route that was circuitous, through streets and alleys that were busy with many other walkers, bikers, and donkey carts. There were a few cars as well, but not many.

I had a favorite house on my walk. A corner house, two storied but squat looking, covered with a cement or stucco that was the same tawny color as the Sahara. I liked it because I was reminded of a prairie style house I knew in the town where I grew up in Iowa, but mostly because of the porch filled with geraniums. It was unusual to see such a porch in Cairo, where almost all the houses were walled along the street, but there was a wide, welcoming entrance to this house, ablaze with red and green plants; geraniums that never seemed to stop blooming. They were on the sides of the porch as well as on shelves that rose to the ceiling, a screen of color that throbbed as I walked past. I liked to walk home mostly to see that porch and the beauty of the geraniums that were so generously displayed there.

....

The Cairo Marriott Hotel is a mix of the old and, for Cairo, the newest. It joined a palace that was built at the time the Suez canal was completed, housing the Empress Eugenie of France in those days, with two tall towers erected on either side of the wide back garden and connected to the palace by walkways from the main floor. The palace contains a beautiful marble lobby, restaurants, a ballroom at the top, as well as a casino and sitting rooms and wide hallways and staircases. There are more restaurants and bars in the new tower buildings, and all the guest rooms are there, but the main attraction is the lovely old palace that has been fitted out to accommodate the public and guests of the hotel.

I visited the Marriott often. It was just behind All Saint's Cathedral on Zamalek, the church I attended and where I was the pianist for hymns on Friday mornings. Sunday is a workday in the Muslim world, and we attended church on Friday, the Muslim holy day.

Before I went to church I often stopped at the Marriott to get coffee and a muffin—my Friday breakfast—at the Bakery Cafe in the hotel. The coffee, which they called American, was not the best, but the place was pleasant and very clean, and I enjoyed sitting at a table watching the hotel guests come in to buy picnic lunches or breakfast. I went there at other times; school holidays, some Saturdays, and whatever odd chance I got, because I liked the atmosphere and the resplendent gardens just down the stair.

Sometimes I met friends and we went to Harry's Bar, a comfortable room in the base of the north tower, for their fried chicken—an all you can eat buffet kind of thing—that was cheaper than almost any other food I ate in Cairo. It was tasty as well, and could be enjoyed with the best of brews from Harry's.

....

All Saint's Cathedral holds a lot of memories. When I see its picture, I am immediately taken into the place and can *be* there in many ways. The cathedral brought me the familiar, the things I was accustomed to experiencing in church, and a sense of home. The Anglican-Episcopal service is the same worldwide, or is supposed to be at least, and I found that it was in Cairo. We had the same lessons each week that would be heard around the world, many of the same hymns were sung, and the prayer book we followed was very like the one I had brought with me.

I am Episcopal by choice, having found that particular church when I was an adult. I genuinely appreciated the balance—spiritually, historically, and philosophically—of the service, and it was what I thought a church should be. I had been organist in varied denominations before I became organist in an Episcopal church, and my experiences often left me concerned about the way churches functioned—why they did the things they did, and what they left out. I didn't wonder about the Episcopalians. They didn't seem to leave anything out. I had found my church, and quickly became a part of it.

When I went to Cairo, I wondered what I'd find there and thought that perhaps there would be no church at all. Instead, I found All Saint's Cathedral and its priest and parishioners who were welcoming and kind. I was very grateful.

....

Faluka. Falucca. Felucca. There are many ways to spell Arabic words when they are translated into English. The fact that Arabic doesn't place vowels into words and that some of the sounds are spelled differently in English make the translating difficult. I chose the spelling "faluka" because it best represents the sound of the word to me. And I think I like the tall letter "k" rather than the two "c's" in the usual alternative spellings.

In any case, a faluka ride is a must if anyone is in Egypt very long. A faluka is a small boat that can hold about fifteen people at most. It has a big triangular sail, and as it catches the wind and moves along the Nile there is little that can be more pleasant after a hot day in Cairo. Falukas have been around forever, one of the oldest of sailing vessels, and they move with great speed when the wind is right. I have been on falukas in Cairo, Luxor, and Aswan, but my favorite place to ride in them is Cairo. Perhaps it's simple nostalgia, but I like the width of the river just between the islands of Roda and Zamalek, where most falukas sail. It seems like an inland sea there, with the shore on both sides so far away. The buildings of the city and the noise of traffic are almost removed from the picture, and the sound of the water is strong and appealing.

I went for a first faluka ride shortly after I got to Cairo. We sailed out to the center of the river and ate a picnic while we watched the distant shore and heard the water against the hull. The air was much cooler out there on the water, and the picnic was altogether a refreshing time, one that I was fortunate enough to repeat rather often.

....

The new Cairo Opera House is located in Zamalek, close to the Cairo Tower. The old Opera House, which was located in Midan Opera in downtown Cairo, was destroyed by fire in 1951, and the new house was built nearly two decades later.

The buildings are designed with familiar dome roofs, following traditional Middle Eastern architecture, and are the same color as the desert, more obviously so than most of the city. They are large and can accommodate crowds, but fit into the landscape without effort. Surrounded by wide walkways and lots of green spaces, lawns, trees, and shrubs, the house is peaceful and the complex harmonizes with itself and the river which flows close by.

I didn't go to programs there very often. They didn't offer much western classical music, and I didn't have much understanding of Arabic music, then or now. That is a difficult music to comprehend without a lot of study, and I didn't take the time to do that, unfortunately.

The primary attraction of the Opera House for me was the setting; the domed halls, the lighted walkways, the large lawn bordered with green palms, and the river flowing past—an Arabian Nights scene, if ever I saw one.

....

The offices for the company I worked for were in a commercial building in Garden City. There was a bank on the ground floor, our offices on the first (American second) floor, and other offices and businesses above. I'm not sure how many floors are in the building, but believe that six or seven would be about right.

The building was fairly new, with very modern architecture, and flowed along one of the curved streets of Garden City, an area near downtown Cairo with serpentine streets that look like well rounded X forms, connecting to Sharia Al Qasr Al Aini as it extends south from the downtown area.

The bank on the ground floor was a busy place, and I was made very uncomfortable every time I went there by the open tables of money that lined the center walkways of the bank floor—customers and bank employees passed close beside them constantly. Different currencies were represented, but much was in Egyptian pounds, and sat there, apparently unguarded, while everybody passed along beside it.

The tables held neat stacks of bills, all sizes of bills, about eight inches high per stack, and they covered the entire table top. Not all banks displayed their money that way, and I was a little unnerved to walk among those tables. It seemed, to my western mind, a blatant challenge to would-be robbers.

The truth is that no one in Egypt is likely to take any of that money. The penalty is severe—sometimes the removal of the hand or the head of the offender, depending on the amount of money taken. Punishment is also swift, often within a few days. I am sure that there were security measures I knew nothing about, but I still was uncomfortable.

I didn't do my own banking there. I had to take my checks, one in U.S. dollars and the other in Egyptian pounds, to the banks they were written on because I had no bank account in Egypt and couldn't get one—I was not Egyptian. For me everything was always a strictly cash transaction. I thought they took a long time to cash my checks, and they did, by U.S. standards, but I learned later that Egypt has a relatively fast system compared to other countries where I lived and had to do banking every month.

....

The office building was directly across from an apartment building, one with attractive balconies above the street level. The balconies were large and partly walled with thick cement, but they were deep and shadowed throughout much of the day. As the afternoon wore on, the westering sun eventually entered and found the interior wall, filling the entire balcony with light.

There was a woman, an elderly woman, who kept a large group of birds in one of the flats on the first floor of that building. Every morning she brought the cages out to the balcony, with the help of her maid, and set the birds in the fresh air. They were beautiful birds; we could see them clearly from our office windows, and she fed and watered them and cleaned their cages while they were outside. She took most of two hours a day to do this, and she repeated the routine every time I was in the office in the morning.

Parrots and macaws with bright green and blue plumage, fiery red headed green birds, white and black macaws and yellow large birds with black on their wings. We got a good look at a wonderful avian collection that was treated to the best every day.

....

Old Cairo, the Christian sector of the city, has two of the oldest churches in the world, St. Sergus and St. Mary's. St. Sergus, the oldest church, was founded in the fourth century to honor two soldier martyrs. It is entered below the street level, indicating age but not importance. The crypt beneath the church, now often flooded by Nile waters, is believed to be a place where the Holy Family—Mary, Joseph, and Jesus—stayed for awhile when they escaped from Bethlehem into Egypt. The crypt is the original church, but the upper level was built on top in medieval times.

I stood at the top of the stairway to the crypt, trying to visualize what lay below, but water filled the entire area and I couldn't make out very much. As far as I know, there is no proof that the Holy Family stayed in that place, but Egypt is a land with a long memory, and I tend to think of it as a true site. The church is a good place to visit, however, because of its historic value, and some very old icons and interesting wall paintings inside.

St. Mary's is more interesting to many people because it is still in use today, and because of a strange folkname, "The Hanging Church." To many Westerners that name conjures up a very different idea, but no, the hanging part means "suspended," as in being partly without a substructure, and that is exactly what it is—St. Mary's is built on top of two Roman towers, which strongly support the building. The entire thing is sitting on the towers that lie beneath the front and along one side. Much of the nave has no substructure, hence the name. The church is supported only by very old, very heavy beams.

St. Mary's sits high above street level, due to the fact that it sits on the towers, and is reached by a rather long and steep flight of twenty nine wide steps. The church is filled with art and glows from many candles that burn along the altar and in niches of the building. The icons are beautiful, Byzantine in appearance, and many are old. One of the oldest screens in the church is from the twelfth century, and the oldest icon is from the eighth century. Some even older articles that were in the church have now been sent to be displayed in the Coptic museum nearby.

....

There are several pyramid sites in Egypt, the most famous being the complex on the plateau west of Giza, on the edge of the great Sahara Desert. I must present only a quick mention here, or an entire book would become necessary, because these pyramids are so beyond comprehension that they more than deserve to be called one of the few wonders of the world—both ancient and modern. To say that they are fantastic, or incredible, or even unfathomable does not seem enough. They, like Cairo, simply *are*.

The first time I saw the pyramids in real life I had gone with a group of fellow teachers during the first week I lived in Cairo. We went out late in the day in order to see them and planned to stay for the Sound and Light Show that is held in English several nights a week. We rode in taxis, and as we looked over the rooftops of the city out on Sharia Al Haram, with about three miles to go, one of the women in the car shouted, "There they are!" and they were indeed there, ahead on the left, their pointed tops hard against the sky. That was my first impression. They looked hard. No pliant outline against the blue horizon, they were made of the same stuff as the Sahara itself and seemed to stand defiant against time and sand.

After we arrived at the ticket station along the road, bought our tickets and drove up close, the pyramids had changed to become monster walls that, when standing directly under, did not seem pyramidal at all.

We drove around the road that went past them, up to a place called the panorama, where we saw the pyramids with the city of Cairo behind them, then back to a parking lot to begin a trek around the base of the largest, Cheops, which is on the east end of the line of three. (This is the pyramid I could see out the western windows of my house, but I could not see the others because they stood in line directly behind the first, and he overlaid the entire view.) It took over an hour to walk around Cheops, and it was thirsty walking. I drank the entire contents of the water I had brought and was needing more when we got into the taxi, drove down the slope past the Sphinx, and stopped at the Sphinx Coffee Shop, a small place that sat under the plateau hillside and close beside the right front paw of The Beast. The pyramids loomed above us like three generations of a family that bore a striking resemblance to each other, which, in a sense, they were.

The Sphinx sits in a hollowed area; the rock was removed in ancient times, cut away to reveal the body of the lion, while large stones comprise his haunches and feet. He is surrounded by a wall, a high wall, so that it is difficult to find a place to look over and peer at his lower portions, but from the coffee shop terrace, and especially from the rooftop viewing area, everything is clear.

The Sphinx is probably my favorite monument in all of Egypt. The large beast can be seen in his entirety from many angles, and is more in scale with humans than the immensely grand scale of the pyramids- whether at Giza or Sakkara or other locations—and the Temples of Karnak or the Valley of The Kings. The Sphinx is approachable, if not actually friendly, and does not intimidate the unfamiliar visitor as does the vastness of the other structures.

We had cold drinks in the coffee shop, looked around the small gift shop area, and then climbed to the roof to see the Sound and Light show as darkness began to grow. The arena where most visitors see the show stretched out in front of the coffee shop to the base of the wall surrounding the Sphinx; hundreds of chairs in long lines. How fortunate I felt to be on top of the coffee house then, and even more so when a small truck came down the path between the rows of chairs, fogging the air with insect repellent just before the spectators came in to take their seats.

A small amount of repellent found its way to the rooftop, but most of it hung in visible form around the chairs. Then the tour buses arrived, people started coming in, and soon the show began. The show had its better moments, but the most interesting aspect to me was the light flooded pyramids and Sphinx, especially the silhouetted settings, when they seemed to brood in the red or blue lights as a mysterious voice discussed the mysterious ways in which the pyramids affected everyone who saw them. They really do, of course, but the Sound and Light show did little to enhance the mood of the pyramids, although they tried.

The next morning I awakened to large red welts left by hungry mosquitoes who had escaped the gas.

I dutifully took all my guests who came to Cairo to that show, but found it a bit too artificial for my own enjoyment. I would have loved to go to the pyramids on a moonlit night to see them with the stars overhead, but they were safely locked and guarded, except for the viewing area in front of the Sphinx Coffee House, but that was open only during the show.

Sakkara, the site of the wonderful Step Pyramid, is older and just as interesting as the Giza plateau. The Step Pyramid, also called the Pyramid of Zoser, was the first attempt at building a pyramidal shape, so far as archeologists know. Built in the ancient *mastaba* form (rectangular structures with flat tops), each mastaba a little smaller and built on the top of another, until the shape emerges. This was the burial site of the Pharaoh Zoser, who can still be seen in statuary form, peering through his viewing hole toward the eastern sky in a small chamber at the back of the pyramid. The wide area in front of the step pyramid is fenced with ancient walls, and the sand is swept and clean across this huge front court. Although the pyramid was robbed long ago, its magnificence remains, and that is what a visitor experiences while standing in the front courtyard.

Awe inspiring is too weak a sentiment, but that is perhaps the best description of the place. The court is entered through a partly fallen funerary temple, a long thin building with many side rooms and roof supports with a narrow central passage that leads visitors to the court facing onto the pyramid itself. The funerary temple and its spare entrance to the pyramid court was, for me, a time tunnel that transported me to the ancient world. No matter how ruined the temple and the pyramid may seem, they are still standing in their original configuration on their original soil, and facing them there in the bright sun reminded me of the numberless days they have sat, silent and waiting through centuries and millennia for the world to see and perhaps understand a small part of the greatness they represent and the wonder they have always inspired.

Another extraordinary area in the Sakkara complex is the Serapeum, the underground catacomb where the mummies of sacred bulls were embalmed and entombed. The sarcophagi for the bulls are immense, but there are no mummies there now. A walk through the catacomb on a hot day is refreshing, however. It is very cool there compared to the sunlit grounds above, and gives the impression that an underground garden may lie just ahead, cool and lush with papyrus and lilies.

....

The Khan Al Khalili sprawls across Islamic Cairo on both sides of a major street, and encompasses so many small alleyways and streets that it is very likely impossible to see everything the souk offers. Khan Al Khalili is the largest shopping bazaar in Cairo, and one of the largest anywhere in the Middle East.

Some of its alleys are so narrow that a person can stand with outstretched arms and touch the buildings on both sides, but I have seen motorcycles head down those alleys as though they were thorough-fares. All the passages are jammed with shops of every kind. They are against the sides of the buildings, under colorful awnings that are usually torn, sometimes ragged, and the bright displays of each vendor are festooned over the entire covered area. They hang on racks and wires, and are suspended overhead as far as the vendor can reach with his collecting pole.

There are areas for clothing, carpets, perfumes, food, spice, house-hold goods, metals, gold and silver jewelry, antiques, auto parts and more- all there in great and colorful abundance. The place is busy all day, but comes even more alive at night as the air cools and people are able to come out to find the things they want to buy, and to bargain with the salesmen. It seems almost a game and is fun to watch. There is rarely a customer who leaves a serious haggling session without the desired purchase in hand.

And there are people. The Khan is the only place I have ever ex-perienced pedestrian gridlock. I had gone with a friend, Nadi, and his cousin Muhammed, to the area on the first night of Ramadan at about midnight, and we sat outside a large mosque on the outer fringe to have some food at an improvised cafe. There are supports that are similar to flying buttresses to hold up the old walls, and a TV stood on the end of one of those. The eyes of the men in the cafe were fixed upon it. The TV was playing a video of women in very abbreviated clothing, mud wrestling, and the men who watched were enchanted by the spectacle. Such a thing would never be seen on a public street in Cairo under most circumstances.

We ate our food and then wandered toward the street that led into the Khan. As we moved along the crowd grew closer and I lost contact with Nadi and Muhammed. Everyone was pressed together, unable to step forward, backward or sideways. I stood there, concen-trating on breathing and trying not to notice that I was caught tightly between the men who stood all around me. There were no women in the crowd—they would not or could not get into such a situation. I looked over the men in front (I was a little taller than most of them) and found Muhammed. Nadi could not be seen, but I knew he was nearby.

It seemed a very long time before the crowd began to move slowly, but to move, and we inched forward along the street. I saw a cross street coming up, watched for a moment, then shouted at Muhammed to go to the right, and he did. I pushed and worked my way to open a path and followed him. Nadi came too, just behind me. He had been there all along, he said, watching out for me. We walked through a shop and out to another street. I was lost, but my friends knew where they were going, and gradually we worked our way out of the Khan and found a cab on the main street at a taxi station. We went back to my house and had a good laugh, some tea, and a long conversation.

....

In the King James Bible there is a reference to Gehenna—a place where the fire burns forever. It is a euphemism for hell—and I found it in the Mukottam Hills above Cairo, toward the east.

The day was hot and the climb was a long one, up a narrow sand track past a lot of shacks and huts surrounded by piles of what looked like garbage, going toward a place where there was a large column of smoke rising from the ground. An open sewer flowed downhill along the street, and things generally looked and smelled quite dismal. I was told by a companion that this was a Christian sector of Cairo, the place where the Zabaleen—garbage collectors—lived, and that there was a workshop at the end of the street where they made crafts from the recycled garbage and sold them. I was looking for braided rugs, the very large kind I had seen in houses in the city, and this was one place where I thought they might be.

The rugs were beautiful in a very homecrafted way, and many were ten by twelve feet in size and some were even larger. They were made of various fabrics, all dyed to match, and some had patterns—

stripes and squares—set into them. Most importantly, they lay flat on the floor, including the uneven cement tile floors I had seen them on.

The bus, one of the few I had ever taken in Cairo, had stopped at the last station on the road below, close to the Muslim cemeteries where squatters lived. I hoped that I could get back to it easily, or find a taxi to take home, but for now the only thing to do was walk on up the hill between the piles of refuse that were the cause of the terrible odor.

The higher we got, the bleaker the place became, and there were no more bushes or trees, just rocks and sand and the garbage piled between the huts. The smell began to overpower everything, and the air, acrid and smoky, joined with the column that rose high above us. It was like a fog as the smoke flowed down toward the city below.

I had thought it would take longer to get to the top, but suddenly we stepped across as the road turned to the right, and there it was, the pit of Gehenna, lying open before us.

I was not prepared for anything like it; a deep hole, a very deep hole, that seemed cut into the earth. The distant side was formed by the rocks at the top of the Mukottam Hills, tall and straight, soaring above the hole that lay at our feet just beyond an old and inadequate chain link fence with many torn-open spaces. This was, in fact, an extraordinarily ancient quarry, one of the places where large amounts of the best quality limestone was dug out and cut into blocks to build the pyramids. But when I looked that day, I hadn't yet discovered what the pit really was.

The ground in front dropped straight down a cliff more than two hundred feet deep, and far below in the bottom of the hole, a single bulldozer, still yellowish after long service, was pushing some of the day's garbage dumping into a fire that licked around the blade as it consumed the refuse that absolutely no one could use. Everything that was possibly useful had been removed and stored in the sheds at the other end of the pit, or in the spaces between the huts along the road.

A foul smell rose from the pit. A smell of rotten meat and other food, with overtones of chemicals and possibly even oil. The air was hard to breathe there, and I wanted to get away as fast as possible.

The whole thing seemed terribly efficient because there was nothing left but some ash after the fire had been put to the unusable garbage. The refuse of a huge city was constantly being sorted and saved or incinerated here at this pit of Gehenna, but even that dreadful place had redemption. The leader urged us on, and we walked toward the right, still following the road. Then we saw a rooftop ahead, just over the top of some of the Mukottam rocks on the safe side of the pit. We walked just a little further along, and saw the rest of the building.

It was made of the mudbrick common to the area, a large, white-painted house, with flowers and bushes growing along a path that led to the front door. There was no glass in the windows, but they were shuttered with the typical wooden shutters found all over Egypt. The smell and the heat easily entered the building, but as we went inside the air seemed cooler and the smell less noisome than on the road. There were two large workrooms and some smaller spaces that opened off them, filled with tables where people worked at various crafts and construction. The place was clean, cleaner than most workspaces I had seen in the city, and there was a pleasant aroma that attempted to cover the awful smells that came from the pit just across the road.

We were offered tea, and we had some, as well as some good fig rolls, and talked about the crafts that were made there. Unfortunately, they had no large braided rugs, not even small ones. (I learned later that a village called Kerdassa northwest of Cairo was the place where they were made.) I found some wooden carvings and a few woven pieces that I bought, made a donation in a jar beside the door, and we were off down the hill, moving along quickly to get away from the stench.

On the way down, I had the misfortune of stepping into the sewer along the street, and I was glad to get back to the bus station where I found a taxi to take home, instead of trying to ride the bus again with an uncertain feeling that I might have to leap from it in my soggy shoe when I got to my station.

The Christians from the hill have been the garbage collectors for the entire city for many decades, but in very recent years the governates of Cairo and Giza have contracted with some foreign businesses to collect and dispose of garbage, and to keep the streets cleaner. Everyone receives the new garbage bill every month but this system has not worked well, and many people in the city have returned to the Zabaleen to collect their garbage every week, paying for both services. The Zabaleen have also been hired by the new companies to sort the garbage, which is done far from the hill where they live. So the Zabaleen have ended up with a dual garbage sorting situation, and more and more have returned to the hill to work rather than travel across the city into Giza to work for the new company. The long trip to Giza is altogether inconvenient, and the problem of deciding between the dual garbage collection systems is still in developmental stages. It may be that one day the Zabaleen will no longer sort garbage on the hill, and will have to close the workshops and other self-help programs they have developed. I hope that will not be the case.

The bill for the new garbage collecting system for each family in the two governates is relatively small, but many are refusing to pay it. Cairo was very dirty before, but is just as dirty now, despite the extra street sweepers who are working for the new company. The new system hasn't made any difference in the amount of street fires where garbage is burned on site, or the amount of debris that remains in the public areas at the end of each day. The stairwells of buildings are no cleaner, and the city looks as it always has, littered and unkempt in many places.

While I lived in Cairo, the Zabaleen, represented by two very dirty children, came to my house twice a week and took whatever garbage I had, as well as baksheesh to take it away. I usually gave them a small amount, perhaps fifty piasters (something like seventeen cents—which I had been told was fair in that situation), but after going up the hill to the craft house I was much more generous and they came to my door much more often.

Schools

$\mathcal{I}$ WORKED WITH TEACHERS IN three schools on a weekly rotating schedule. I spent three days a week at the largest school, and one day at each of the others. I really loved the schools and appreciated the teachers I met there. When I say schools, I mean the people and the classes, not the physical buildings, which were in sad condition.

I went to meet the department head and faculty of the first school I worked in before the beginning of the term. I arrived with the administrators of my program, took a long look at the place, and hoped for the best.

The building was in serious trouble. It was a four story cement shell, with open, gaping windows that had no glass. The stairs were narrow and twisted up to each floor, causing traffic jams because there was only one set of stairs for each large section of a U- shaped building. The place would have been a fire trap except for the fact that there was very little to burn. Everything, including the floor was grey cement, and looked like a long abandoned factory. It was, in reality, a third world school. The other schools I went to work in were in better condition, but this one needed help.

There was a gate, a large, rusted iron gate with a few holes punched in it, that stood open the first day I was at the school. It wasn't open very much after that. In the morning as soon as the whistle blew and the morning files formed, the gatekeeper closed the massive iron thing and locked it. After that, if anyone wanted to get inside, Mustafa, the gatekeeper, would peer through one of his peepholes, and if he recognized the person knocking, he opened the gate just enough to let him or her enter. The tight control of the gate prevented "escapes"—students who would try to run through and get outside whenever the opportunity presented itself. Attendance was taken for the day during the morning forms, and if someone got out after that, they might not be listed as absent. All the perimeter walls were built high around the school for that reason, and in that particular school, shards of broken glass were imbedded into the concrete that topped the brick of the walls.

There was a second gate on the far end of the school ground, and I never saw it open, but I did watch as some of the older boys climbed up onto the roof of the bookroom next to it and leaped to the top of the gate and then down to the lane that ran along the wall outside. That was a great game to play on a pleasant day in Cairo. Fahmy Buli's Day Off.

The classrooms were large enough to hold about fifty students per room, with one electric light hanging from the center of the ceiling. The open window at the back let in insects, at times the wind howled through, and during storms the air was gritty with the sand that piled up in drifts in the corners. I looked more carefully at the window frames and could see that they had, at one time, held glass. A teacher later explained that when the students broke a window it was not replaced, and that after the first few months all the windows in the school had been broken. A broken window meant that all the glass was removed to avoid injury, with only bits clinging to the frame where the glass had been glued. In winter these rooms could be very cold on a cloudy day, and we all shivered and covered our heads.

All the rooms but a few were the same cement grey, and the desks, the only furnishings, were crudely made of green two by six boards.

They had been hammered together with large nails that were often sticking out or bent and pounded sideways into the wood. Each desk was built for two, but some of the older students fit rather too tightly. As a final touch the desks had been brushed with a small amount of varnish that didn't cover the entire piece, which probably would have looked better without incompleted varnish anyway. The biggest problem, though, were the splinters. Each of the seats had a great potential of slivering—the wood was often broken and shredded into the beginnings of slivers along one edge, and the slivers looked sharp.

The few rooms that were painted looked a lot better than the cement, but the furniture was the same. A smaller number had curtains that could be pulled across the window, and some of the girls brought their own cushions to sit on. The students had bought the paint and done the work themselves in order to brighten the room they would stay in all day, every day, for the school term. In Cairo the teachers rotate and the students remain in the same room. That arrangement avoids crowded passages and stairways most of the time, as well as meetings between the sexes, which many people considered to be the highest priority.

Another, more unusual situation occurs when a teacher is absent. There are no substitute teachers in Cairo, so if there is no teacher for the next hour, the door is simply locked on the outside and the students are allowed to do whatever they want inside the room. (That is how all the windows got broken so soon after the building was opened.) Generally speaking, the teacher who comes in after that has a bad time bringing the class under control again.

The most curious thing in each room was the blackboard. In reality there was none, but a large part of the front wall of the room was painted black. The teachers wrote on the black wall with a chunk of very soft chalk, which made a small pile of dust along the floor underneath.

There were wings for the boys' classes and for the girls as well. In that school there were few coed classes, although some schools had begun to have boys and girls together in most classes as they got older. The sexes did meet during lunch breaks, but there was always much supervision.

Inspectors. That one word can create anger, fear, annoyance — or respect among a faculty. Each governate has a crew of inspectors who make the rounds visiting schools to make sure that everything that should be done in the classrooms is being done. Some inspectors want to look at minutia, others take a more general view, and still others care nothing about what's going on in the classroom with the exception of three all-important items: 1.) The expression, *Allah Akhbar*, must be written in Arabic in the center at the top of each chalkboard wall in every classroom every day, 2.) The date must be placed at the top of the right hand side of the board, and 3.) The name of the textbook with the current page number under discussion must be at the top of the left side of the board. That is all some inspectors require for a teacher to get a good report written about his or her work.

The catch is that the textbook page number and the date placed together on the wall need to agree. In Egypt there is a requirement for all teachers of the same level class to be working on the same textbook on the same page on the same day as every other teacher of the same class at every other school in the nation. That may seem a highly undesirable goal, and it is, but there are school districts across the U.S. that are currently adopting that kind of regimented, thoughtless ruling. Teachers, however, invent ways to cope with the situation. I worked with many teachers who wrote the required information on the board but *did* something entirely different on a daily basis. They did this calmly, without much thought about the rules, realizing that a teacher should not be so controlled by brainless bureaucracy which kills the creativity of the teacher and students as well. Inspectors often overlooked such a digression, and some didn't even seem to realize what was happening.

A few inspectors were respected because they were realistic. They treated teachers and students well, and made helpful suggestions

when they were appropriate. They sat in the staff room and had coffee
or tea as much as they spent time in the classrooms, and developed a
working friendship with the staff. They become one of the teachers,
and were not feared because they could give a bad report. They didn't
need to do that if they did their own jobs well.

The schools follow the old British system in many other ways.
Classes are divided into forms rather than grades, everyone wears a
uniform (with modifications for those girls who need to wear more
coverings), each day begins with a rigid flag salute in the central quad,
and rather formal exams are taken at the end of each term.

Teachers trade schools for the exam days, to prevent cheating, so
far as I could tell, and we weren't allowed anywhere near our school
or the students we had worked with all term. Instead, all our teachers went off to a school across the city to monitor exams there. (I was
not included because I had no classroom responsibilities of my own.)
After exams were taken, we went into an otherwise empty school (no
students) and the faculty worked for two days marking the exams
and rewarding everyone with the grades earned on what she or he
wrote.

The tests had been prepared by the faculty, then typed and printed on two old copying machines that filled an entire room. They were
collated and locked away until an unknown staff from another school
unlocked the cupboard and handed out the exams. I am not sure
about the length of time students were given to write each part, but it
must have been adequate because there were many good and several
excellent essays written during those days.

We worked steadily at reading and consulting and considering
marks for every student, no easy job, and no one took the work lightly.
Every teacher had gone through that system, and I sensed that they
placed themselves at one with the students much of the time during
marking days. It was also a test for the teachers. If most students in a
class did poorly, it reflected on the teacher, and that would then become an issue. Getting the negative attention of inspectors was not a

thing that any teacher desired or needed. The day by day routine was tense enough, but any special attention or extra supervision could become a serious matter.

Marking days were also filled with humor and camaraderie. We laughed at small things during that time, and chatted as we worked. We were loose and free and I soon understood why everybody had anticipated marking days. We sent two of the group out for our lunch after deciding on what kind of food we wanted, and everybody paid their share, a thing that they had not often let me do. I was considered a "guest" most of the time and I felt that they had not fully accepted me until they allowed me to pay my own way. Soon after that they let me take my turn at buying the daily tea or coffee for everybody in the staff room, which I enjoyed doing far more than they ever knew.

I have a lot of respect for those teachers. They did absolutely tremendous things with almost nothing to work with, and despite the very low pay and the difficulty of living in Cairo on such meager salaries. I always think of them fondly, and can easily forgive some of the things they did in order to make a living.

One of the teachers had been at the school from the first day. He was the only one in the English department, as far as I knew, who was part of the original staff. When the school opened it was small, but had grown to more than 2000 students in less than ten years. He had a large responsibility; he alone handled the distribution of the textbooks for most of the classes. He worked out of a large bookroom, a shed, really, attached to the back of the school building, and stored all the books for all of the classes there, a big job for a school that size. Of course, he was paid more for the additional work, but even that was hardly an incentive for handling all the books.

In the Experimental Language Schools education is not free, so each family must pay a fee for the semester tuition to the local school administration office, but the books were sold out of the bookroom, and the person in charge was responsible for collecting the fees and sending them to the local office. Gilel, the book man, did this twice a year, and he always sent the funds to the office promptly.

One day when I arrived at school I heard that Gilel was in great trouble. He had been called to the administration office due to a discrepancy in the book prices. I didn't understand exactly what that meant at first, until a friend on the staff explained. Gilel had, over the years, gradually added a small fee—his own fee—to the price of each book. It was a very small increase at first, but as the actual prices of the books went up, so did the inflated fees for each book he sold. He had done this for several years, and his "take" must have been rather substantial. I didn't understand well enough to get the whole picture, but I knew that he could be jailed or fined, and greatly humiliated, along with his entire family.

I was worried. I had been a guest in his home and knew all his family. The day of reckoning came, and when I went to school Gilel was there, a little subdued but quite unscathed by any punishment. The administration had forgiven him, had forgotten his theft, and he was once again in charge of the bookroom and fully accepted as a teacher at the school. I was a little surprised but very relieved at the solution they had come to, and we never again heard anything about it. I am also sure that Gilel priced the books more carefully after that.

The foundation I worked for placed libraries in many of the schools where the mentors worked. The libraries took a lot of planning and many meetings to get under way, but a new library filled with English language books as well as a new copy machine was an important asset to the school.

I was told that none of the school staff could do the work of building or setting up the library. Egyptian employment laws are strictly worded, although not often enforced, but the foundation wanted everything to be done according to the law, so we had to find carpenters to build shelves, someone to install new floors, electricians, a place to buy the copier, and a plan to order books from publishers according to faculty selection. Much of that was easy enough to arrange, but there were varied opinions about the copier and some of the furniture, and there was a lot of discussion about book selection. After gathering all the information I could, I ordered items and acted on what I thought was best for the entire school.

There were many rules to follow—the new copiers could be used only in the library for library purposes, the books must be selected by a committee of teachers, and we would have to hire all the building and installation of furniture and equipment from outside the school. One of the staff members, Ahmed, told me that he had a neighbor who was a fine carpenter, and that he could bring the man to meet me and that he—Ahmed—would interpret the conversation between us.

I met the man, who looked a bit questionable, but decided that if he produced the work and it was good, I would have no problem. He and Ahmed measured the space, and worked out a crude drawing of the shelves that would line the room. As the deadline for the installation of the shelves came closer I asked about the progress and the carpenter came to the school again and told me that they were nearly finished. I was satisfied, and went ahead with the other things I needed to do for the library.

On the day the shelves were to be delivered I asked Ahmed about the time they would arrive and he hedged, saying that the carpenter had not been able to finish them yet due to family problems. After waiting a few days I asked again. He gave the same answer—the shelves were not yet finished.

About two weeks after they were due to be completed and installed, the shelves arrived at the school one morning still slightly tacky from not-quite-dry varnish. The carpenter delivered them, and with the help of another man began fastening them to the walls. They looked fine, so I paid him, and thought that was the end of that part of the project.

The next day, another teacher who worked in the department came to me and told me that it was Ahmed who had built the shelves, and that the "carpenter" was someone he knew, who received baksheesh for pretending that he had done the work. The informant had seen Ahmed collecting the funds for himself from the would-be carpenter as he left the school grounds. That was another lesson in the Egyptian economy and how it functioned. I felt a bit disadvantaged, but only because I had been so naive.

The most common thing that teachers do for extra money is to teach private lessons. Nearly every student at the secondary schools where I worked took private lessons, and some of the older students wanted me to teach them. They thought that private lessons with a native English speaker who also knew the school system and worked with their curriculum would help them in their exams, but I had been warned not to accept any private students. The company stressed that policy, and despite some parent encouragement and good offers, I didn't get into that business.

I realized, however, that some of the teachers who did well with the private lessons feared that I would be competition, so I made it very clear that this was not an interest of mine, and that the company forbade any outside work, including private lessons, and kept to my word.

Teachers are paid a bonus for working regularly, as well as the standard government wage, but still fall short of enough money to live comfortably without needing to take under-the-table pay for extra jobs that come their way. Private lessons are, for them, a lucrative and honorable solution.

The teachers I knew who taught private lessons had only a small business most of the year, but about six weeks to a month before exams, they had all that they could handle, and worked until midnight or later with small groups of students to make sure that they would do well on the exams. Some unscrupulous teachers (none that I knew, however), left out some important information in the daily classes and told their students that if they wanted to get "all" the material, they would need private lessons because there simply wasn't enough time during the school term to teach everything. They did their small share of business, but those who worked steadily and taught everything required were flooded with requests at exam time, and they could name their price for assuring parents that their children were ready to get high marks on the exams and advance to the next form.

There were other money making schemes that went with private lessons. Some teachers home-published workbooks and sold them. These books accompanied the lessons they taught, or other teachers could use them, or students could have help at home with the books if someone there knew English reasonably well. The books were published from mimeographed pages, on the cheapest paper, and the ones I saw were filled with errors.

There is a great investment of time and money in a student's examination preparation, and it must pay off because it is a standard part of the process that determines a young persons university training and future.

....

There are many educational conferences in Cairo, a city that is proud of its universities, which number at least five, all very large and important in that part of the world. The largest of these is Cairo University in Giza, with more than 200,000 undergraduates enrolled. With so many large universities, it is inevitable that conferences of all kinds will arise, however lackluster or truly dull they may be.

I have attended too many conferences, a problem that is frequently part of the expectations for a foreign educator who lives in or even visits Cairo. One of the first was a conference held in Nasr City, a suburban area northeast of Cairo, which was sponsored by the Ministry of Education for teachers who were teaching in English language schools. There is a large conference center, beautiful and new, a showplace for all kinds of meetings that needed a better facility until that one was built. We met there, a considerable distance away from the most congested parts of the city.

There were mostly Egyptian teachers present, with a number of native English speakers as well. After the first speaker had finished there were questions posed, and sometimes attempts at answers given, but mostly the questions were asked by academics who wanted to be seen and heard, a situation endemic in academic communities worldwide. One question that was under consideration was whether the English language had become too invasive in the Middle East, and could, therefore, cause changes in the culture of Arabic speaking nations.

There was one professor, however, who took the podium with considerable pomp to emphasize the need for knowing English, and knowing it very well. "It is essential," he thundered in an impressive display of sound and determination of spirit. "It is essential that we know the language of the enemy!" He had made his point and left the podium. Most people were silent, a few applauded, many were shocked, and some later apologized to me and some of the other Westerners present. But the thing they all knew was that we were the enemy in the minds and opinions of some who were there, as well as much of the population of the Arab world. They usually treated us well, but we were still the enemy. It took a couple of years of increasing friendship and lots of discussion for my closest friend in Egypt to finally tell me that he could really, truly trust me, and added that I was like a father to him. That remains one of the finest compliments I have ever received, but terribly poignant due to his sudden death a few months later.

The daily routine at each school was much the same; preparing for and attending classes with teachers, discussing the class at a post-mortem (an after class evaluation), planning future activities, coordinating efforts between teachers, and answering questions from many of the faculty about the English language; grammar, usage, and structure.

Most questions were sincere, but a few were designed as a test. I spent a lot of time fielding questions about the U.S. and education, the life of a teacher there, and how I came to be in Cairo. I talked with them about school buildings, students, and all the things that we all knew well. I also shared in tea and coffee drinking every morning—usually two or three times- which is a very important part of Egyptian culture. An old saying goes that when someone has eaten bread and salt with another, they are somehow more closely bonded. That applies to tea and coffee today.

One of the people who figured importantly in the coffee and tea culture was Om Arabia, a felahin woman who made the drinks in her cubby near the English language staff room. She had a small gas ring where she heated the water in tiny pots that she held by their long wooden handles over the flame until it was boiling. Then she poured the super heated drinks into small glasses, grounds and all, placed them on a tray with her asbestos fingers, and headed down the corridor to deliver them before they had a chance to cool enough to handle. I learned to hold the glass by the heavy bottom rim and the very top, sipping the scalding coffee slowly on the opposite side. I never dropped a drink, but came close a few times. The drinks were always presweetened, and I ordered *mas buut*—not too sweet—but they came with loads of sugar anyway, as any self respecting Arab would prepare or drink tea and coffee.

Om Arabia was a proud woman. She would always greet me the first time she saw me each day with both hands above her head in a sign of respect. I greeted her with a smile because she was always so cheery, and we had a good relationship almost all the time. The great mistake I made—that caused her to become angry with me—started out with my desire to eat whatever food I brought to school and to drink the coffee she made, on a clean surface. The tables in our staff room, in every staff room, were covered with dirty oilcloth. Om Arabia was also the cleaner who went about with a somewhat rancid rag and wiped the tables every day, or when she saw something spilled on them. No one seemed to notice that they were slightly tacky and covered with stains that should have been washed away with clean water and soap.

One day I decided to have a go at cleaning the oilcloth on the table where I sat—we had unofficially assigned places in the staff room—and brought a container for water, soap, and a clean cloth to school. I had just completed the job—which had transformed the cloth into a clean, dry surface—when Om Arabia swept in to inspect the results of the insult she had heard about. She looked at the table, then at me, and began a snarling diatribe that grew ever more shrill, then she began to sob, and finally, large tears ran down her face and she left the room in croaking sobs and moans. I had never experienced anything like that, and stood dumbly beside my clean table, feeling the greatest remorse. I was truly sorry that I had offended her. I didn't touch another table, and never repeated the insult again. Rather a dirty table than an angry Om Arabia.

As I left that day, she was waiting for me beside the gate, tears gone, but still furious. She shouted at me and gestured in several ways that were suggestive of curses, and I apologized to her in the best Arabic I could. It made no difference. It was at least two weeks before she would serve me coffee again, and she refused to even look at me as I passed.

When she finally brought me coffee one day, I rewarded her with a huge smile, a hearty Shokran, and a very large amount of baksheesh. It took some time, but the smiles accompanied by the baksheesh paid off, and she returned to her normal style of greeting and even brought me some of the bakery breads that she sold—as a complimentary treat. Of course, she was more than rewarded by more baksheesh, and in the end, when she heard that I was leaving, she cried again, this time because she said that she would miss me "too much."

Eternal Cairo

ALTHOUGH CAIRO ISN'T THE oldest city in the world, it is very old, and has risen from the past without sacrificing its oldest self. The city goes on living in a kind of renewed incarnation with each succeeding era. Cairo is both impossible and improbable, but is as strong today as in the past, incorporating the very newest into the already existing mega-metropolis, and there is always a sense of the past clinging to the stones, wherever one goes in the city.

Some of the newer suburbs sit on ancient grounds, where temples and palaces and long vanished houses once stood, and where apartment blocks filled with families and hope for the future are fixed to the land today. The oldest parts hold streets and buildings that were much the same long ago, even as much as an entire millennium in the past. The oldest mosques and churches still witness to their grandest days, and the oldest houses are filled with families, some directly descended from the original builders who lived there more than five or six centuries in the past. This is indeed an old city, and although many things have changed, the spirit of Cairo, the collective memory of its ancient history, is palpable in the Cairo of today.

Cairenes are watchful, alert people, and nothing much gets past them. Subtleties are useless there, for the most part, and while the people take life in stride with certain expressions, *ensha'allah*, for example, they are also very sensitive to any rude or dismissive treatment, as we who are from the western world are sometimes predisposed to give. Ugly Americans? Often we can't enjoy a place like Cairo because the city is not what we think it should be. To the Egyptian, that seems to be a bit much from a nation less than three hundred years old, world power notwithstanding.

There are certain things that come to my mind as I think of the eternal qualities of Cairo. None of them are the ones we go there expressly to see; the pyramids and other ancient monuments, or the Nile, or the museums. I think instead of things like facilities (toilets, really), families, food, friends, romance, taxis, and weather. A bit more earthy, but also the stuff that real life and a colorful history are made of; things we aren't always aware of, but things that are essential for happiness and well being.

Taxis? Yes. Taxis. They may not seem eternal, but people have always had to get around the city in some way, walking or riding in or on a vehicle of some kind, and taxis are only the most recent incarnation of transportation that is affordable to many people, and readily available.

There are *taxis* in Cairo, perhaps simply thousands, but more likely, multiple thousands, and sometimes it seems that there are almost as many taxis as people, at least until the people come out in force in the evening. These taxis are affordable, especially for Egyptians who pay half or less of the fare that is required from foreign riders. But even with inflated fares, I could go anywhere I wanted in most places in the city for about four to six pounds. That is less than two dollars at the top price. The only places that were more expensive were long trips, to Maadi, or to the pyramids, or Kerdassa. Those cost more, but I could ride on the Metro to Maadi for less than three pounds, and the Metro was faster and a bit cooler, too.

Early in my stay in Cairo, living in the hotel, I took what I thought would be a short ride across Zamalek without negotiating the price in advance. When I got out the driver asked for "six bounds." I had paid only three or four to go all the way to Garden City and knew that six pounds was too much, so I argued and told him that the price should be only three pounds. He was adamant and demanded "six bounds" again. (There is no "p" sound in Arabic.) I wasn't at all sure what to do, but thought I was a victim of the concept that all Americans were rich, so I insisted on only three pounds. I might have gone to four, but he was so belligerent that I held my ground.

I had been advised by some Americans who had lived there for a few years that taxi drivers try to take advantage of foreigners by demanding high fees, so I finally left the three pounds on the seat and got out. He chased after me for a short time, shouting "six bounds" loudly, but gave up, got back into his taxi, threw the three pounds out of the window, and went off. Someone else picked up the money. I felt defeated, and was concerned that I might have made a mistake.

I had. When I got back to the hotel I asked the desk clerk, who told me that a small sign posted beside the door said that all taxi fares from the hotel began at six pounds. After reading the sign, I always paid at least six pounds whenever I took a taxi from the hotel stand. If I wanted to go only a short distance, I went to the corner and hailed a cab from the street and paid only three or four pounds. I never encountered that particular driver again, but I learned that Ugly Americans could come in all varieties, myself included.

Cairo taxis are black and white and very small. They are almost all Fiats, made in Egypt at an earlier time, and therefore can be bought and sold at the cheapest prices. A peculiar thing is that they all have meters, but no one ever uses them because they were set by government standards years ago. The cost at that time was so little that no driver could possibly make a profit these days by using the meter, which, I am told, cannot be reset. (There could be a large study of the thought processes of government and the Egyptian people involved in this, but I cannot go into that here.) The government has recently replaced the meters, but the price still has to be negotiated ahead of time in order to avoid an angry haggling at the end. Drivers seem to prefer the haggling to the metered fares.

Some visitors believe that they should pay whatever the driver asks. They would do so out of pity, but that isn't always the best motivation. It seems a good idea for people with incomes that are commensurate with western living standards to pay more, and we always have. The unspoken rule among most Egyptians is that we should pay more because we have more, and taxis always do cost more for Americans. Drivers are adept at spotting us.

I rode in taxis all the time, some days taking more than six trips, and learned the rates quickly. I walked around my neighborhood, but whenever I went to places I didn't know, or places that were too far to walk, I took a taxi. I never had to wait; there were always more than enough cabs on the streets.

Once I asked a driver to take me to my street, *Sharia Musadaqq, gamb mustashfa ibn sina,* but he took me to a dark nearly rural street on the edge of the desert and smilingly announced that we had arrived. I told him "No, keep driving," which in Arabic is *"La-ah, alla tuul, "* with a slow horizontal motion of the index finger. He turned around and headed back, found *Sharia Musadaqq,* and let me off in front of *mustahsfa ibn sina*—Brothers Of Sinai Hospital—without any explanation as to why he had taken me nearly into the desert. I had some dark thoughts about that, but let it pass.

....

The weather in Cairo is often monotonous, but there are times when it takes on new vigor and becomes a problem, and other times when the weather is a delightful and beautifully unexpected blessing to all life in the city.

Every spring the *khamseen* winds blow around and above the city, coming in from the Sahara, and sending a fine silty dust over everything, with great increases of temperature and dark sunblocking clouds of sand. The sand doesn't usually blow through Cairo; the winds are high and overhead, creating a sallow sky and dust that leaves a dirty film on every surface, including skin and hair. There is almost no air movement on the ground, but the darkness and heat combine to create a sense of foreboding that can go on for days.

Khamseen means fifty, and it is within a period of fifty days in the earlier part of spring that the dust comes. On one day the air can be soft and the sunshine almost a cool radiance, unlike most of the year, but the next day turns sinister, yellowed, and hot. The first time I experienced the khamseen winds, I dreaded going outside into the street. Visibility was considerably altered, and even the tops of tall buildings seemed in a fog. After four days the storm ended, and the air returned to its soft springlike self, and no spring I have seen anywhere was more beautiful.

Everyone thinks that Cairo has no winter, but it does. Not winter in the same sense as the more northern parts of the world, but the cold is intense for several weeks, and clouds come in with a thin wind—but not much dust—and there is no heat in most buildings.

I slept with two heavy blankets, one wool, in order to keep warm at night, and had to wear a long scarf that I wrapped around my head when I was at school because the air was so cold. Sometimes the sun shone weakly, and we left our staff room to work outside, sitting along the southern wall of the school building where heat reflected best. Even in full sun I never got too warm on those days.

Christmas time is in the middle of the cold season, and the evenings were cold enough to wear a sweater or a coat as I made my way across Zamalek or Dokki. I found an Egyptian Christmas tree—there were many for sale at floral shops; tall rather fernlike plants, and took it to some friends who had invited me for Christmas Day lunch. That was a full Christmas feast, and we spent the day eating and singing and talking, a wonderful celebration despite the fact that I was so far from family and home.

The cathedral was dressed in greens with red ribbons and candles for the Lessons and Carols service, and the familiar music, sung by the largest congregation I had seen in the place, was strong and full, reverberating into the open central spire that rose high over the nave. Church has always been the place where I celebrated Christmas most deeply, and I found that true in Cairo, also.

By the end of January the weather was warming again, and soon the hot days of spring—and summer—and autumn, were renewed. Cairo is hot most of the year, but is not usually unbearable. The unbearable heat comes as you travel south into upper Egypt.

I have often said that it never rains in Cairo. That is largely true, but not entirely. The first year I was there we had a scant rainfall one evening. Rain made the streets slick and mud dripped from the trees, but it didn't last, and the next day was as though nothing had happened.

During the last year I lived there I went to the U.S. during the early part of April for a convention, and when I returned to Cairo a strange event began to unfold. At first I saw it at night as flashes of light over the distant Sahara. Lightning, I was sure, but far away. Each night the storm moved closer, coming eastward very slowly, until on the fourth night it exploded in the skies above the city with great bolts of lightning and tremendous thunder claps, the loudest I had ever heard, echoing between the buildings. I opened all the curtains and watched—electric storms are fearfully fascinating.

After the lightning had moved slowly toward the east I heard a new sound. A sizzle. It became louder, and soon rain fell in torrents. I watched, but the city was darkened by an electric failure and I couldn't see much. I eventually went down the hall to go to bed, but stepped into something wet. In the dim light I saw a dark stain of water that flowed across the floor from the window, and settled into a pool in the center of the room.

I tried to mop it up with towels but there was too much, and the rain continued to pound against the window. I finally got into bed wondering what to do, but whatever that was had to wait until morning.

When I awoke I saw the extent of the damage. The wooden floors had turned dark in places, and there was still water standing in the center of the floor. The windows had been closed (to keep out mosquitoes) but the water had seeped in through large openings that were hidden by the window frames. The force of the wind coming from the west had driven the rain through those openings onto the floor. There was a little water in some other rooms, but the greatest damage was in my bedroom.

Although the time was early, I called the owner of the flat. We had been on excellent terms since my first early call about the lack of water, so she was grateful and said she would come and check the damage as soon as she could. I left for school then, not knowing what to expect when I got outside. The rain had stopped long before, but the sky was still cloudy.

I couldn't find a cab for a long time, and I walked out to Sharia Musadaqq before I finally flagged one down. There was water flowing slowly through the streets, mostly along the sides now, and water sitting in large puddles in any low place. There were few cars on the road that morning, but the puddles splashed high up under the taxi and the driver was fearful of getting his car swamped in the flood. There was almost no one walking along the streets, a great contrast to the usual morning activity, and when we got to the sandy lane that led down to the school, the driver could turn and go down, getting me as close as possible to the gate. The lane was usually clogged with pedestrians.

I walked along on the edge of the lane, through the gate and down to the school entrance. It was locked. I banged on it a few times and Mustafa came through the water, unlocked the gate, greeted me with "*sabaa il heer*," and smiled intently as I stepped inside.

I entered and stood amazed. Instead of the wide sand quad in the center, there was a lake with ripples crossing the surface. The crew was busily sweeping water out of all the lower floors into the lake, which readily absorbed whatever water they could sweep into it. I went into the English staff room that was still partly covered with the flood, and two men were there pushing the tables to one side so they could take out the carpet that lay under about two inches of water on the floor. There were no teachers or students around. I realized then that no one else would be coming, so I went back out to the street, picking my way past the deepest puddles, to a large hotel coffee shop that was close by, and had breakfast.

The storm was all that anyone talked about for days, but the evidence of all the rain disappeared quickly. By the next day the water had gone from Cairo and the sand looked dry again, but upper Egypt had been hit even harder, and the torrents flowing off the desert had toppled many houses along the river. They were made of mud bricks because it *never* rained there. The bricks at the base of the houses washed away in the heavy rain, and the rest of the house caved in. That storm was called a "hundred-year deluge." Nothing like it had happened in more than fifty years, and nothing like it was expected to happen again in anybody's lifetime.

....

Facilities in Cairo vary from the hole in the ground to the deluxe public restrooms in the best hotels, complete with attendants who hand out individual towels to each patron. *Baksheesh* necessary. The towel was extended with one hand while the other was presented beside it, palm upward. A gentle smile was also included in the exchange, and a polite *shukron* completed the transaction. It was always a pleasant experience.

There were some places I knew where the situation was far different. One of them was the men's room at the school where I spent the most time. The room held one sink, old and greying from collected dirty handprints and whatever else. There were solid doors on the front of two stalls. The doors had bolt locks inside, but no toilet paper at all. Egyptians actually frown on flushing paper down toilets and almost everyone uses the wire—a form of bidet—instead. The facility itself was a hole in the floor. And there was no wire, either. The hole was good-sized, and was kept reasonably clean, and it even had a flushing device on the wall behind it, but it was not easy for me to use if I had to have any toilet experience beyond urination. I was careful to take care of morning ablutions at home and hoped that nothing more would occur during the day at school. But once or twice I had to cope.

In the grand hotels, patrons were handed two squares of toilet paper if they requested them, so I usually carried my own, as most expats do. Those pocket sized packets of tissue are a great boon.

Restroom experiences varied with the establishment. In one large coffee shop downtown, the men's room was attended by old women. Men were using the cubicles, to be sure, but some were using the urinals along one wall while the old women cleaned the floors and empty stalls and handed out paper towels. (For toilet paper we had to depend on what we brought with us.) In a society that is so modest, it seemed strange to see that sort of thing commonly accepted. Perhaps it's my western prudery.

....

Food is important to everyone in Egypt. The rich have certain foods that only they can enjoy, but everyone, from the felahin to the rich, loves *kosheri*. It is called the Egyptian national dish, and is made of macaroni, lentils, rice, and garbanzo beans, covered with fried onions and a spicy tomato sauce. Kosheri is a cheap vegetarian dish on the one hand, but also a wonderful eating experience, delicious in its many styles, and served in homes as well as lots of places that sell only kosheri. I went to a kosheri place that was known as the best in Cairo with friends sometimes, and the food was good, but the price of a meal was astonishing—less than a dollar for a huge serving of the stuff.

Everyone can eat in Cairo because basic food is very inexpensive. Beggars and the poorest folk can all buy bread, a delicious flat bread,

that is eaten with kosheri or vegetables. Government controls on prices of certain staple foods have allowed everyone to get tasty nutrition
and have enough to eat every day. The felahin are happy because of
these laws, and everyone can benefit from the low cost of food.

Some food, however, is very expensive. Meat is at a premium, and
anything that is imported is also costly. There are expensive French
bakeries and patisseries in the city, and I sometimes ate at restaurants
that would be considered expensive anywhere in the world, but that
was not my usual fare.

I ate no meat at home, but did have some once in awhile when
I was with friends or in a restaurant. Most of the time my diet was
made up of local eggs and vegetables; things that I could clean in my
sink and store in the refrigerator. I also bought cheese—but it was imported from Europe, as was the wonderful French butter—and local
bread from a great bakery near my house. There were stores in neighboring Mohandeseen where I could buy canned goods and some fro-
zen food. Those things are what I cooked with and ate at home, and
they were mostly inexpensive and readily available.

At times I was a dinner guest at an Egyptian home, which was a
rare and wonderful treat. The houses I dined in were not the richest in
the city, but they laid an astounding table, both with the quality and
quantity of food and elegance of table service. The china and flatware
were the very best, and the table linens glowed under the light of
candles standing in tall silver candelabras. Flowers and other dinner
guests completed the picture, and we spent hours at the table, eating
slowly and very, very well.

All the food was prepared and placed on the table before the
guests arrival, so the hostess was at the door to greet us, and we sat
and talked for a short time—until the dining room door was opened
and we were taken inside. The sumptuous meal had many courses, to
be eaten in no particular order. There were beautiful *mezzas* (salads
of various kinds), baked pasta dishes and several meats—lamb, beef,
and chicken—with vegetables and potatoes, fish with Egyptian style

rice, many kinds of breads, all followed by pastries and fruit desserts. We had tea to drink, as well as fresh bottles of water. Usually the meal ended, hours after it began, with chocolates and coffee. I wish I could say that I enjoyed those banquets as much for the conversation and conviviality of the company as the food, but in all honesty, the food was always the star. I can't even think about eating that much anymore, and wonder that I ever could.

I usually had breakfast at a hotel or restaurant on my way to school, or at school in the teacher's room, then went home and made lunch, and fairly often would go out in the evening with friends or go alone to eat in a restaurant. I sometimes had a poor meal in a restaurant, but I chose carefully, and was mostly satisfied with what I ate in Cairo. I did develop a craving for pork because there was none available in most of the city, but one cafe in Zamalek was known for pork dishes, and I went there to get sausages with pomme frites or with eggs and toast, sometimes. The place was only in Zamalek then, but has recently spread across the city with other outlets to satisfy the western craving for good pork sausages.

There is a Muslim holiday called the *Eid Al Adah* that comes seventy days after the end of Ramadan. This holiday commemorates Abraham's sacrifice of a ram instead of his son. The son of sacrifice that Jews and Christians name is Isaac, but Islam believes he was Ishmael. On that day families who can afford a lamb or an ox bring it to the front of their house to offer to Allah. After the animal is slaughtered they butcher and divide it among the family and the poor.

For at least a day before the Eid, the animal is displayed on a tether in front of the house, and the poor go around the neighborhood seeking the best animal. On the morning of the Eid they line up on the street and wait to receive a portion of the meat from the sacrificial animal they have selected.

I watched this process from my window high above the street for both days because the Eid is a national holiday, not understanding exactly what was happening until the animal was ritually offered.

The beast fell amid shouts and cheers. To my amazement, the men in the family took this animal—a very large ox—into the house, and emerged onto the roof with it a few minutes later. They spread long sheets of butcher paper on the roof and proceeded to cut the animal into many pieces. The crowd waited below, quiet and steady, as the men worked with the meat. After nearly two hours, they had cut and divided the meat into portions, wrapped it, and carried it downstairs in large tubs. Everybody swarmed around the tubs, and soon they were walking away with a wrapped piece of meat in their hands. Everybody in Cairo must have had meat to eat that night.

....

People watching is a sport that seems a bit unsavory to the Arab mind, but people watching is an exciting and interesting pastime in Cairo, with throngs of humanity pouring through the streets at all hours, all apparently impersonal toward each other, but cleverly hidden sidelong looks can often be detected, aimed toward any person who is unusual or interesting. Many times I have glanced up to see someone who seemed to have turned his eyes away at that moment. And at times I have heard my name from beside or behind me, and as I looked, a friend or an acquaintance would disengage himself from the crowd to come alongside and walk with me.

I got to know a good number of Egyptian people rather quickly in Cairo because I worked with them every day. I met the English faculty at my school, but also all the other faculties—math and science and social studies, as well as everything else that was a part of the school curriculum. I knew them mostly as acquaintances, but some of the men on the English staff became friends, and Nadi, an English teacher, became my closest friend in Cairo.

Another teacher, Achmed, from a different school, became a close friend as well. Achmed and Nadi were from the same village in Al Minya, in upper Egypt south of Cairo, but did not know each other there, at least not well. Nadi was Islamic, and Achmed, Christian. That difference alone created a gulf between them that could not easily be bridged except in a city like Cairo.

Achmed told me very little about his life in Al Minya, but Nadi liked to talk about his family and home, so he told me quite a lot about them. His father was a village chief, in the tribal tradition, and had at least three wives that I heard about. Nadi had many brothers, and several sisters, although I was told very little about women in his family except for his mother. It is an offense even to ask about the health or well being of another man's female relatives. Mothers are an exception to that rule because there is an attitude that everyone will respect your mother, and she is, therefore, safe to mention.

I met one of Nadi's brothers, a young secondary student, also named Achmed, who came to visit, and a cousin, Muhammad, who wrote Arabic poetry—considered a very special art—and was in religious studies at one of the prestigious Islamic Universities in the city. I heard a lot about Nadi's other brothers but never met any of them.

Achmed lived in a flat near Sharia Al Haram with three or four of his brothers—or perhaps more, I was never sure. There were twins— one was a physician and the other in banking—an older brother, also a banker, and a younger boy who was still in university. I never did recall their names, but had met them on a few occasions when Achmed came to my house with one or more of them. Mostly, he came alone, or was there with Nadi.

At times, I met my friends for dinner, or one or the other would stop by my house late at night—late for me, anyway—and sometimes one or both stayed overnight because our conversations lasted so late that morning and school were almost upon us before we knew the time. Once Achmed stayed for a week because he had no water in his flat (I'm not sure how his brothers managed) but Nadi stayed only rarely.

Over many months I gradually came to know Nadi. He always seemed to be open and eager to know people, but he didn't often talk about himself or how he thought and felt about things. He smiled all the time, but behind the smile was an angst that at times erupted into focus.

He had a hard life as a youngster, a childhood with older brothers who were difficult to get along with. He was the son of his father's second wife, and all his older brothers were sons of the number one wife and mother in the family. Although he didn't ever say as much, I had the impression that the first wife, who always has preeminence in Islamic family hierarchy, didn't like Nadi and taught her sons to treat him badly. His own mother, being in a secondary role, could do little to help. Nadi left his village at a young age, eleven or twelve, and ran away to Cairo where he worked hard every day to survive. He carried heavy hods of brick, a job that caused him a lot of back pain in later years.

I don't know why he ran away from home, although I can guess, but when he returned at age fourteen he was apparently more able to take care of himself. He never did tell me much about that, but became very quiet and moody when he mentioned it.

He had a sense of doom that hung about him despite his usually cheerful disposition, and would often say, even with a smile, that he knew he would die young. His ambition was to become a professor of English language and literature, and he had set out a plan that would take him to his goal, but he felt that he would never live to accomplish it. I got a bit impatient at times and assured him that he could do what he wanted if he worked through the plan. My confidence in him seemed to help, but he gradually became more morose over the time I knew him in Cairo. When I left Cairo I felt that he was still tenuous although he tried to be cheerful.

Friends and families are often intertwined in Cairo. Your closest allies are almost always members of your own family, and they remain close all your life. Women develop a new familial loyalty when they marry, and to a lesser extent men do as well, but original family connections remain the most important friendships that anyone can have, even after marriage takes place.

Families change over time, and although there are many newcomers to a family group through marriage, the greatest changes come through death. Egyptians have a rather peculiar way of handling death. They are terribly emotional and grief stricken for twenty four hours, but as soon as the requisite mourning time is ended, most are able to get back into their lives without the pressures of remaining in a grieving process; but widows are not so fortunate.

Widows are expected to grieve for a much longer time, an indeterminate time for many, and to wear the black of mourning for years to come. Of course, women tend not to marry again after the death of a husband. This is a sign of great mourning; that the widow cannot imagine having a happy home ever again. She must always mourn her loss. While others—children, brothers, and the rest of the family—get on with ordinary life, a widow must show respect for years, continuing in a brooding silence most of the time. Anything less would be disrespectful to her late husband, and his family (children, brothers, sisters, and parents—if they are still living) will not allow her to forget for a moment that her proper place is among the permanently mournful.

Ramah, a young woman who worked in the company office, lost her husband rather suddenly due to an error made by doctors when he became ill. She was, truly, overcome by grief, but as time passed she recovered somewhat and began to talk about her future. She and her two children lived with her in-laws, and they encouraged her to continue in a state of mourning for months. When she finally decided to wear something other than black, her mother-in-law was upset, and told her so.

I talked with Ramah about her situation, even suggesting that she should try to marry again—to find a suitable young man who had lost his wife—but she told me that her in-laws would never allow that. She could not break free from the conventions that held her, and she remains an unhappy young widow, although she does have the reward of two wonderful children and is always grateful for that.

....

Hospitality is important in Egypt, and I was invited, several times, to go to someone's country house for a weekend, often by someone I hardly knew. What I did know was that country houses had primitive facilities and virtually no bathtubs or showers, which I thought essential in the great heat from the nearby desert, so I tended to stay within my own comfort zone. I always managed to find a good reason for not going, although staying at home was my true objective.

The company I worked for dissuaded travel to the villages or governates in the Al Minya and Assuit region. Those were the areas where tour boats were fired on, and threats were made against Western people. The company determined that it was not safe, but did allow some of its employees to teach at a university there. Those men could travel, usually by train, into upper Egypt, but all the rest of us were discouraged from going to Al Minya and the surrounding area.

....

Romance beckons in Cairo in every season, and is one of the most discussed topics among all kinds of people, also one of the least acted upon. All the young men I knew asked my advice about romancing their ladies or finding someone to romance, and they were all obsessed with the idea and the ideal of love, but seemed to enjoy the miseries that romance placed upon them even more than the realities of loving and being loved.

A young man may see a girl in a shop or on the street or, as I have been told often, riding on a bus. He talks to her, but usually doesn't sit beside her, and asks her if he can telephone her father. If she gives him her telephone number, she really means that she will agree to marry him if her father agrees. That's all there is to it? No, there's much more.

The young man must call her father if he is serious, and then he makes an arrangement for them to meet, if the father agrees. If, after the meeting, the father decides that the young man is suitable, all is well and the couple is engaged. They can, within limits, meet and walk together along the corniche or in a public garden and talk about their future life together. They must not, however, under any circumstances, be alone together in a private place. That is forbidden.

Usually these romances are nipped before they can start to bud. Sometimes the girl will not give a man her phone number, but if she does the young man may never call, or her father refuses even to meet him, or they may meet but the father refuses to allow so much as a discussion about potential marriage. Romance has many pitfalls.

Despite all the problems that can short circuit amour, thousands of young couples in Cairo are involved in a romance, and they walk sadly along the corniche, unable to so much as touch or hold hands, but they do place their heads a bit closer together than is proper at times. They are sad because, although they are engaged to be married, they must wait, even for several years, for the marriage to take place.

The rules for marriage are strictly observed. A young man must have sufficient money to buy a flat to live in and to furnish it completely for his future wife before a wedding date is set. He must also have a certain level of savings and income, prescribed by her father, and there are other, varied hoops he must jump through in order to obtain final permission to plan for a wedding. The father of the bride holds all these things in his hands, and he is often very picky about the details that he demands in order for a man to marry his daughter.

Sometimes dowries must be paid or gifts given, and sometimes the father changes his mind about the amount of income or savings a son-in-law must have prior to marriage. If a father wants to complicate things or postpone a wedding, he has all the power to do so, and no one can change that.

Despite all that, weddings do take place, and new brides are inducted into their husband's families at a great pace every year.

A bride may finally prevail and persuade her father to allow her to marry, only to exchange his dominance with another; that of her husband, and sometimes his father as well. Women are not without recourse, however, and they have subtle ways of dealing with men which they learn at an early age. They may seem demure at first, before the wedding, but a bride may change into a lioness soon after the vows are made, and scold and control in so many ways that no man can be a match for her. Eventually, most women control the home, although men pretend that they have the final say.

A highly intelligent and educated woman I knew slightly displeased her husband because she insisted on doing something that he did not favor. Because of this he soon told her that he was planning to take another wife, as four are allowed legally in Egypt. She then set out to dissuade him from doing that while she worked to attain her own goal. She made his life a living hell, in a benign sort of way, confusing him and "forgetting" things, nagging, howling (tears and all), and cajoling until he relented on all points. She got what she wanted, and he remained cowed for the rest of the time I knew them in Cairo. Women do have power if they know how to use it.

The most important rule is that a young woman must be, absolutely *must* be, a virgin, or, in rare cases, a widow. In our time virginity is easily enough determined by a doctor. A female doctor, of course. I am sure that there were methods of confirming virginity in the past, but can only imagine what they might have been. Virginity is required for marriage in both religions, Muslim and Christian, and although the men are supposed to be virgins as well, there is a wink and a smile which indicates that a man is better off if he has some sexual experience in his history.

A young man I know, a Christian, came to me one day filled with smoldering anger that seemed about to explode. He told me that he had just learned that there was a surgery that women could have so that no one could know whether she was or was not a virgin. I asked him why that was so important, and he went into a rage. "I can't marry anyone unless I know that she is a virgin!" he shouted. This is the same man who told me that for several years, beginning when he was fourteen, he had an ongoing sexual relationship with an older woman who lived next door to his family. The woman's husband worked in a city some distance away, and lived there most of the time, but while he was away she "needed attention," so had recruited him to help her. I tried to point out that his was a hypocritical position, but he could only respond that he had felt that he was doing a good thing by helping the woman, and that she had taught him everything she knew in exchange.

Young men have presented themselves as miserable—in love and unable to obtain permission to marry, or in love but unable to collect the resources the woman's father demands, or in love but unable to persuade the object of his affection to allow him to talk to her father. (This is only a problem if he doesn't know her family.) All these things are part of the romantic picture in Cairo, and some are ways that women use in order to establish themselves in a man's eyes as an equal, or at least nearly so. Unfortunately, equality usually ends the moment the wedding ceremony is completed.

There was a young woman, a teacher in one of the schools where I worked, who was very beautiful, modestly dressed with all the requisite coverings, and able to talk freely to me and to other men on the staff. She was bubbly and laughing, friendly in a polite way, and apparently unaffected by the gulf between the sexes. I was invited to her wedding but didn't attend, primarily because the husband seemed very distant and watched her interaction with me and all the men from school with scowling eyes. Another American was also invited, and he tried to get into the wedding but was turned away by the guards at the gate.

As soon as she returned from her honeymoon she would avert her eyes and speak only the polite minimum, most traces of her former personality gone. Her husband, or perhaps her mother-in-law, had apparently told her how to behave, and she lost the sparkle that made her the lovely person she once was. She remained closed and wistfully unhappy from that time on.

Young men, especially, are often morose about romance, and can sit and sigh and otherwise convey their misery in silence for long periods of time. This behavior is common in Egypt, and I have seen it repeatedly on TV shows that are rather like American soap operas.

During the first winter I was in Cairo I spent many evenings alone at home, and turned on the TV for company although I didn't understand the language. There were only three channels, all Arabic speaking. I started watching a "soap" on one channel, and there was a new, apparently live, installment every night during the week. The plot centered around a young, beautiful blond woman who was an American, happily married to a young, dark and handsome Egyptian. They lived on the family compound in the delta north of Cairo, in a palatial house with multitudes of servants. The American woman was a look-alike Shelly Long, and that alone was intriguing. Despite all the servants on scene, Shelly cooked and cleaned and served and helped, all the while looking lovely in designer dresses—modest designer dresses, of course. Her husband had a younger brother who figured prominently in the plot. He was in love with yet another beautiful woman, an Egyptian, who wore the coverings but managed to show some strands of silky hair and an ankle once in awhile.

The problem, among many others in the story, was that the Egyptian girl's father had refused to allow his daughter to marry the young man, and he, the young man, would sit alone in his room at night, staring at the wall or out the window, looking as though he would prefer death. All these things were conveyed through long, anguished looks and body language, and the situations of the principals. I didn't understand Arabic at all.

Romance changes over time, but very slowly. New ages create different approaches to courtship and marriage, and yet the desire for love and companionship stays the same. A century ago there was no meeting on a bus or walking together along the Corniche, there was only the permission from the girl's father, usually after a discussion with the young man's father, and the marriage was arranged. The young people often had never met and had little to do with any of the arrangements, and that was accepted. That kind of marriage arrangement is still common in some places, but with each decade a few more young people are being emancipated so far as their romances and marriages are concerned. This is happening almost imperceptibly slowly, and young people are sometimes impatient for sudden change. That will not occur, as they know, and there is a restless stirring in youthful society over the matter.

If there really is a "dark time of the soul," I think that in Egypt today it could be the time when young people are carefully and painfully negotiating their marriage contracts and trying to find their own happiness in the mine field that surrounds Egyptian Romance.

Physiognomy

*T*HE NILE FLOWS THROUGH the heart of Cairo, amid the noise and confusion that tends to nearly engulf the city, but the water is a peaceful, gently moving thing lapping the shore, sometimes against hard and fixed concrete abutments, sometimes along green swards that contain lawns, benches, trees, and bushes.

The Nile is wide when it flows as one stream that is not divided around the islands. It is so wide that at some points the sounds of the distant shores are quieted, and the sonority of the water is the most prevalently audible aspect of that world. The watery realm reminds us of the pharonic idea that the god Amun created the world from an island in the Nile—a pile of rock, sand, and silt—and that he stood upon it and pronounced the water and the shore and the green valley of the river, the desert, and all the lands that the ancients knew. And, because he spoke it, it *was*, and remained from that time until now.

This creation dream, not unlike other stories of creation that exist in many cultures and religions of the world, is one that deals tangibly with the Nile, the mighty river, and was, therefore, something for the minds of the ancients to grasp rather easily, and to believe. The Egyptians of pharonic times were not derelict in their service to

Amun, and were blessed by the constancy of al nil and the crops and the seasons.

The expression that a picture is worth a thousand words may indeed be true, especially for those who are visually oriented, but I often favor words—words have a way of insinuating themselves into the conciousness more subtly than most pictures I have seen. There are many picture books, sometimes called photo essays, about Cairo, and there are online sites filled with pictures. These pictures can evoke strong memories, but written descriptions, filled with evocative phrases and ideas, create a world that is partly imaginary and partly experiential, whatever that experience may be. We bring ourselves more truly into written expressions than we are able to bring ourselves into a photograph or other realistic representation of a scene or situation.

So it is with my experience of Cairo. I love the entirety of the place, and find all kinds of enchantment within it. I do not, therefore, always want to see the city in hard, photographic dimensions, although I know they are there. I sometimes want to see the softer and gentler memories that I have assigned to the city from the recollection of my own encounters and adventures. The *physiognomy* of Cairo, its countenance or face, seems one of the best words I can find to describe this "picture" of Cairo, to bring it to the fore, and to find the beauty of the city beneath its rough exterior.

The Corniche Al Nil, a street that follows the slow curve of the river, is lined along one side with the best hotels and fine restaurants and luxury apartments that only the very rich can enjoy. They are in early twentieth century buildings that average less than ten stories, apartments above, with wide balconies taking advantage of the riverside location, and the ground floor a shop or restaurant where the better-heeled come and go. On the water side of the Corniche is the green place where couples can be seen discreetly seated just far enough apart on the benches, talking in low voices, living for a time in a world that is distanced from the reality of their everyday existence.

Many bridges cross the Nile. Most are choked with cars and other transport, but there is one certain bridge that contains a wide pedestrian walkway, an old bridge that arches above the river, beautiful and ornately art deco—another place where young couples stand above the circling water and dream together.

Cairo, like Paris, really is a city for lovers, but the best that the lovers can do here is to sit or stand with a bit of distance between them, not allowing the world in, but remaining untainted and above suspicion by their circumspect conduct. A Good Woman does not allow a man to touch her with any degree of intimacy until he is her husband. And a Good Man will never attempt an intimacy that is beyond the accepted Cairene standard of behavior for courtship. The attitude of the city is not conducive to trysting, and the rules are carefully maintained, unless the couple in question has no plans to marry or for their relationship to become in any way legitimized.

It is impossible for Muslims and Christians to marry (unless the Christian converts), thus creating the greatest single impediment to marriage as well as encouragement for illicit affairs. If two people from different religions become enamored with each other, then anything can, and often does, happen between them. Everyone knows that the hidden depths of Cairo hold many torrid secrets.

....

There is an old hotel sitting just down the road from the pyramid of Cheops, and in one of the hotel dining rooms an entire wall, an immense wall, is a window that brings the pyramid right into the room. Cheops seems to be a neighbor's house, although a colossal house, just across the street, but is actually still a good way off. I attempted to walk there one evening from the hotel, The Mena House, and the climb up the grade to the plateau, even with the excitement of Cheops standing before me, was very tiring.

The Mena House is a wonder of a place. It is old, a former hunting lodge for the royals who once ruled Egypt, and the passages and doorways are shaped in marvelous occidental arches and designs. There are new parts, and a large rounded swimming pool, but the character of the hunting lodge pervades the entire setting, and with that there is a nostalgia that is both romantic and exhilarating. The building is of basic desert tan color, several stories tall, although its height is carefully disguised. There are high windows, lots of crescent shaped dormers, and beautifully irregular roof lines. The whole thing is topped with flat roofed towers, two or three, depending on your perspective, and surrounded by beautiful grounds with palm gardens and a multi-arched arcade that sits between the pool and the rest of the complex.

I was fortunate to stay there once, as someone's guest, and have been back many times to enjoy the restaurants and other amenities of the palace. The Mena House is far from the heart of Cairo, and that can be an additional perk for those who like things quieter and the air purer.

....

The heart of Cairo is generally considered to be Tahrir Square, a very large place that lies in front of the Egyptian Museum and behind the Nile Hilton Hotel, with The Cairo American University and the Mugamma facing into the square as well. Tahrir Square is a noisy, oily smelling place filled with pedestrians and buses, and directly below the square is the central terminal for the Metro, where the lines cross and passengers can be taken swiftly away to the far corners of the city.

What is probably the largest bus station in Cairo is located in the square, and that, combined with the Metro, makes it the transportation hub. The Square is huge, but doesn't seem as large as one might expect. There is always so much activity and motion of buses and cars and people that perspective is lost in simply finding your way through it all.

Sharia Tahrir runs along the south end of the square, with the

Corniche Al Nil out in front of the Nile Hilton on the west, and other major streets extend spoke-like from the east side. The area is surrounded by a green lawn with palm trees and flowers, an attempt to soften the paving and the tawny colored edges of the tall business and apartment buildings that surround it on all sides. Nearly everybody in Cairo must pass through fairly often.

There are gigantic neon signs on the tops of buildings surrounding Tahrir Square, advertising electronics and technology, soft drinks, cinema, and potentially anything that a modern city needs or uses to hold itself together. It may not be a lovely spot, but is dynamically dramatic, and to a great many Cairenes represents their city at its best.

....

Sharia Ismael Muhammad in Zamalek is as typical a street as I can remember on the island of Gezira. A street where shops, most of them in half basement places with a short stair down to the entrance, sit below buildings filled with apartments and a variety of other occupants and offices.

The buildings are bland, concrete things that rise abruptly from the entrance edges that face the street, to heights of ten and twelve stories. Some are a bit taller, and some are very tall, twenty to thirty floors of flats in many areas of the island. Zamalek has a tremendous population within its boundaries.

Sharia Ismael Muhammad has trees, lots of tall trees that line the street in small boundary areas along the curbs. The trees are green year round, and have developed a pleached canopy of leaves that covers the street and shades it, while making a veritable bower for pedestrians to walk beneath, and a lovely sight from the lofty windows on both sides. It is as pleasant a place as I have seen in Cairo; a good place for taking a stroll whenever I am in that neighborhood.

There are some old hotels along the street, as well as newer ones, and the guests who stay in them are privileged to enjoy the trees from balconies that rise above the greenery on the sides of the buildings. There are many people in the streets at most hours of the day or night, and there is noise, but the trees seem to add a buffer and create an almost country feeling within this tight place in the center of the huge city. It is one of my favorite streets, in one of my favorite parts of Cairo.

....

I was given a copy of a David Roberts drawing of Cairo from his visit there in 1838. The drawing is of a small section of the Khan al Khalili, near the ancient gate that stands in what was once the city wall. There is a minaret on the left side of the gate (another, unseen minaret, is on the right), an old mosque, now closed and filled with dirt and debris stands on the left in front of the minaret, with a building that once contained fountains of water just behind it. There are tattered awnings extending from a shop building on the right, and quite a number of men dressed in gallabeyas and turbans in the small square in front of the shop.

The gate itself cannot be seen in the picture. It is a huge, solid iron gate that rests on hinges that haven't been moved, so I was told, for over five hundred years. The massive gate is more than twelve feet high, and somewhat wider, and as I recall, it has an overlain pattern that was probably placed there to give more strength.

The picture, however, is nearly the same as what you see there today. A few light bulbs strung along the tattered awnings—very like the awnings in the picture—and some rather garish touristy merchandise that is available in the shop are now part of the scene.

Khan al Khalili stretches in all directions from the gate. It moved outside the original boundary centuries ago, and extends through streets and alleys on both sides of the city walls. Twisting alleys lead to abrupt ends, decaying walls are spread in long lines down the streets, and all is covered with desert dust.

There are old buildings inside the khan, some sitting in disuse, but many extremely old structures are still in use as shops or houses for those who have a stall there. They stand with uneven walls and rooflines, looking as though they might collapse at any time despite the fact that they have been there so many centuries. Many have *me-shrebeeyeh*—a bay window cantilevered out from the wall—covered in delicate wooden lattice work that allowed someone standing inside to remain hidden while looking out through the slats. This provided women a chance to get some air as well as look onto the street and enjoy the passing parade.

Fortunately, Egyptians do not tend to "improve" a place or to destroy what is already there unless they decide to build something new, so we have these old things, unchanged except for the passing of time, that recall the past, a very long-ago past. Much of Islamic Cairo has this character, and the khan seems to lead the way. It is a place of mystery, and, with any imagination, intrigue.

....

Beyond the pyramids on the edge of the great desert is a high place that is called the panorama. From the top of this rise one can look toward the east and see the three pyramids of Giza standing sentinel over the city of Cairo that seems to begin at their very feet. The view ends at the Mukottam Hills that rise on the eastern side of the Nile valley, enclosing what today is Cairo and its suburbs. The panorama has a tremendous vista, and is a separating point between the city and the desert. To the west, the Sahara spreads outward toward Morocco; unrelieved sand and rock except for a few small oases, for nearly two thousand miles.

The panorama seems a bit different when looking toward the west. It is the far point of the horizon from the Nile valley, but the way the sand folds and drifts gives the illusion of greater distance than it actually is.

The first time I noticed the panorama was on my first visit to the pyramids, just days after I had arrived in Cairo. As we were sitting atop the Sphinx Coffee House waiting for the Sound and Light Show to begin, the sun was setting behind the pyramid of Khofu, the central pyramid of the three, and the last blaze of light came from behind its left wall as the sun descended below the rise.

A few minutes later, in the darkening twilight, three men and three camels came wandering across the panorama, slowly making their way as though they were on a long journey, although in all likelihood they were headed home for their evening meal after a day of entertaining tourists. The figures were far away but very clear, black silhouettes against the dying light. The men in their gallabeyas, with tall poles in their hands, leading the long-necked camels across our line of vision. We—the group of teachers who had never visited the pyramids before—were enthralled with the beauty of those beasts and their guides, silently gliding across the distant hill between the points of the two largest pyramids, poetically moving to the pace of the distant past, all provided, apparently, for our enjoyment and appreciation.

....

I traveled in a private car with friends who had lived in Cairo for a few years, and another companion, their friend who had come to visit. As we drove along we passed through the traffic-challenging streets of Giza and continued south on our way to Sakkara, the site of the first pyramid shaped tomb built in Egypt. It is the Step Pyramid, built one level at a time, each level smaller than the one below, until six levels were completed and the imposing shape of a pyramid was formed. That was long ago, about five thousand years in the past.

The Step Pyramid of Zoser, named for the pharaoh who was buried there, is one of the grandest sites in greater Cairo and worthy of as much attention as the Giza pyramids. The place is filled with an awesome light and sense of antiquity that I have never experienced in any other place. In addition, the approach to Sakkara is magnificent, with the heads of Zoser and the other pyramids in the complex rising above the land in solemn grandeur.

The best part of the approach to Sakkara is the Nile valley, the long, deeply green, lovely valley that lies between the outer environs of Cairo and the ancient site at Sakkara. The green fields and trees are an unexpected enrichment, a wonderful sight for the eyes and a deep earthy smell for the nose. The colorful vegetation was not lost on our companion that day, who told us that he hadn't seen anything so green since he had visited Ireland. I chuckled to myself. No one, I thought, would ever believe that on the eastern end of the Sahara desert lies a valley so green that it is favorably compared to Ireland.

The truth of Egypt's great green river valley is strange but beautifully real, and it continues as far down the Nile as I have been, all the way to Aswan, near the southern border of Egypt.

The Nile has a flood plain that is wide in some places, and very narrow in a few, but the river waters the land from beneath all the way, and produces the verdant plant growth that provides produce for the people, and green tropical palms as far as the underground water extends. Even the boles of the palm trees are green in some places, and my estimation of palms changed when I saw them, green and glowing, in the sunlight.

There is a line, though, a literal line, along the edge of the hills that rise along the river. Where the land is flat, there is grass and plant life, but when the land rises, in even a small grade, the green stops at the bottom of the slope, creating a line with a green edge against a tawny expanse that moves away as far as the eye can see. There are a few palm trees beyond the line, their roots extending into the water that is still beneath the ground, but the short-rooted plants do not grow above the flat flood plain line. A little way up the slope the trees stop entirely, and there is nothing then but the sands and rocks that form the great desert.

It is a place of remarkable contrast, and also of notable, natural, green beauty.

There are many places and elements of beauty in Cairo. The ancient places are the first to come to mind, but there are many houses, midans, parks, gardens, streets and even shopping malls that provide beauty in an otherwise unwashed and unkempt place, where the multi-storied buildings and the overcrowded streets vie for attention, and usually win because they are so many. Nonetheless, the beauty spots are there, and when they are found they provide a relief to all the dun-coloredness that forms much of the city.

....

Cairo had experienced a rather large earthquake a year before I went there, and many school buildings were heavily damaged, some beyond repair. I worked in a school on Sharia Al Haram that was meeting in another building after theirs had been destroyed in the quake. The building we were in was a girls' school during the day, but after the girls left at two o'clock, we opened the second shift school at three and were there until nine in the evening. Darkness begins fairly early in Cairo because it is far south toward the equator, so everything was dark by the time school ended.

I was there only one day a week, but the staff and students were so welcoming that I felt a part of the place and had some great times with them. The most memorable was one night when a roving blackout hit at the beginning of the eight o'clock class, and we sat for a few minutes, waiting for the light to come on again.

We soon realized that it was going to be dark for at least an hour. Controlled blackouts are common in Cairo because there is never enough power to take care of the needs of the entire city. At any given time there are areas blacked out for an hour or more.

I was planning to teach a lesson that night. The class was a large one, more than fifty students, both boys and girls. I couldn't see very much and there was no way the students could see anything I would write on the chalkwall, so we went to a discussion of the book we had been reading instead of the lesson I had planned. Throughout that class hour I asked questions and paused for responses. They spoke out one by one, carefully and quietly waiting for each other, responding and asking questions of their own. We had a fine discussion of the themes and philosophies presented in the book while I got a lesson about teaching in the dark.

Darkness, however, is not a metaphor for Cairo. The city sizzles and sings with radiant sunshine, light, and color. In every neighborhood, in every street, there seems to be cause for laughter and a panoply of vivid life. Colors of outlandish combinations glow among the black burkas worn by some women, so the passing people-parade is a joy to watch, wherever one is in the city.

There is a marvelous sense of fun at children's parks, the zoo, or on a vigorous boulevard, that is a great compliment to the city and its people. Cairenes love to play, whether children or adult, rich, middle class, or peasant. I have seen groups of boys playing soccer in the streets, chasing after each other wildly for a chance to kick the ball, as well as adults doing much the same thing on the playing fields at large expensive clubs in Zamalek. In the cafes men laugh and drink tea while smoking the always present shisha, and although the women remain out of sight, at least to eyes of men, I have been told that some women go to ladies' parties where they laugh far into the night. There is sometimes solemnity, but more often irrepressible fun rules the day.

That is the spirit of Cairo, the spirit I recall fondly, and the spirit that identifies a people who are never going to be defeated by life. Egypt has endured, through millenia of change and troubles, and I believe it will endure as long as the Egyptians themselves find joy in living.

Endings

I LEFT CAIRO FOR THE last time not long before the millenium change and the year 2000. I had been living in another city in the Middle East for a while and wanted to visit Cairo again before I left for the U.S., unsure as to when I would be able to return.

I took a taxi from the airport down to the southern suburb of Maadi. We drove along the edge of the Mukattam Hills, just below the citadel, as evening came upon us and the lights of the city spread out across the Nile valley. There were lights above as well, sparkling in the twilight from the Zabaleen areas in the Mukattam Hills, creating a mystique that made it look like a wealthy enclave nestled into the folds of the hills rather than the small huts and piles of garbage that were the reality.

The pyramids were standing, as ever, far to the right on the prominent plateau that had known them for so many centuries, and the reds and blues of the Sound and Light Show on their clear outlines glowed across the valley. There were tall towers, The World Trade Center, Cairo Tower, and the Radio building, all with lights blinking atop, and the sharp teeth of minarets and other lesser buildings were silhouetted against the western sky. Cairo was welcoming me home— once again.

I spent a week visiting places and friends and eating and recalling, until the time to go back to the airport to leave. I went with no sorrow of parting, sure that I would return, although not sure when. It would probably be some time, but eventually I would find the welcome of the city and the warmth of friends—and all that I loved about Cairo—once again.

At the airport I waited for a while in the line to check in for the flight. It was a warm day, and standing in the line was tiring. I finally came to the counter, checked my bags, and was sent on through to the long hall to wait there.

The long hall was filled, absolutely stuffed, with passengers waiting to go through passport check. I had never seen anything like it. There was a long line of women on the right side, and a mass—no line or order in the group—of men who waited, pushing and surging, to get to a position closer to the passport booth. I mentally shrugged and waited, holding back a bit because I didn't want to be trampled in case the mass started moving ahead faster. After an hour we had made little progress, and I had assessed the situation. There were only two passport booths open, one for women, which presented no problem because they were all going through in a neat line, and one for men, chaotic and wild, each shouting and straining to get a place next to the turnstile.

The turnstiles, several of which were empty, were the entrances to the glass booths that were set up across the entire width of the hall. One at a time, passengers entered the turnstile to stand at the window to have their passports stamped. Any open places between the turnstiles were barred with a heavy metal barrier fence, decorative and pleasant to look at, but a fence, nonetheless.

After a while I realized that I would never get to my flight in time. The pace of this process was excruciatingly slow, made even slower by the frequent outbursts of shouting and pushing that the waiting men seemed intent upon. I stood, resigned to waiting, but also interested in the process. Security men stood around, just beyond the booths and barriers, to make sure that no one broke through somehow, and we all waited.

Then things changed. A man had gotten behind the occupied booth and found an open glass panel, probably for ventilation. He reached through and got his hands around the neck of the passport clerk, attempting to choke him. The crowd screamed its encouragement as security leaped across the barrier and pulled the attacker away. The howling was unbelievable. The spectacle was interesting to watch, if I stayed far enough away, but with that crowd and the newest development, I knew I couldn't possibly get through any time soon.

The intensity of the reaction was stronger than I expected. Suddenly, there were people, now both men and women, climbing to the top and covering the sides of the small booth, shouting and banging on the glass, trying to break it open to get the cowering man inside. Security came in force. They wrestled with the mob, and more guards came, blowing into their shrill little whistles and striking with batons against the angry men and the few women who joined them. The melee was interesting, but was soon over. A very large contingent of armed soldiers came rushing down the hall, and there was a quick change in the activity of the crowd.

The men were told to make a line. They did. A different booth was opened, and then another, and the object of the attack was led from his damaged booth under guard. Two more passport men were now available, smiling and ready to take the passports and stamp them. A measure of peace was restored.

After that, under the eyes of the soldiers, the lines moved well, and I got into one, at the far end, expecting more fighting to start at any time. Then, quite a long time before I came to the booth to get my stamps, I looked to the right. The men who were central in the fight, even the man who was choking the poor stamper, were standing at yet another booth, waiting in a very short line to get their passports stamped. They were smoking and talking softly among themselves, laughing at small jokes, and generally having a good time again. They were watched, yes, but they had won the battle. They didn't have to wait as long as the rest of us to get into the boarding area.

Cairo isn't usually unsafe, nor is it unpleasant—much less so than many other places I have lived. In the reality of life there, and in my memory, it was a formative time. Living in Cairo allowed me to learn new things that I had never expected to know, and to live in a new world, a world I could never fully understand or appreciate, but embrace as a gift, and enjoy all that I could of what was presented.

Living in Cairo was also a laboratory. It has given so much information that I will never be able to assimilate it totally. I will make an effort, of course, but there is too much to internalize and re-examine.

....

"Authentic" is a current buzz word that I don't like to use, but authenticity in its simplest form, *genuine*, might work well. Genuine. Not pretentious or ostentatious. Cairo taught me that people can and should be real in their approach and response to living. It is a very real place, presenting a very real way of life. An enticing city that can't take itself too seriously because it has serious flaws, but lives and works well with people anyway. During my first months in Cairo everything seemed unreal; as though it were an invented place for tourists, but that feeling gradually faded with time, and all that was left was the certainty that Cairo was, indeed, real, and that the people I saw every day lived and worked and loved and sorrowed there. In time I could walk outside without staring and thinking that somehow it was not genuine. Despite the disparities, the city must be accepted exactly as it is. Ultimately, that is enough.

My friend Nadi, the young teacher from upper Egypt, always told me that he would die young. I laughed and told him that he was too morbid; that he would attain his goal of becoming a great professor despite his early life, and that he would be known, in Egypt at least, as a man of honor and intellect.

He was right—I was wrong. Nadi died when he was twenty six

years old in a train accident in Al Minya, near the place where he grew up. He couldn't have known, but somewhere within his mystically driven mind he saw the past and the future coming together, and accurately predicted his untimely death.

One day during the summer, which I spent in California that year, I received two letters from Cairo, both telling me that Nadi had died. I accepted the news, but was saddened that I could not have been there to attend his funeral in Al Minya and to see him buried in his family's tomb in the cemetery. To have his friends with him then would have been something that he greatly valued.

A few weeks later I got a letter from another friend, Samir. He also told me that Nadi had died, and that he was absolutely sure that there was no mistake. It was Nadi. Muhammad, Nadi's cousin, had called Samir soon after the accident to tell him. Samir had gone to the morgue in Al Minya himself, a very long way to travel in the night, and looked at the bodies of the dead men until he had found and identified Nadi. There have been incidents of mistaken identification in cases like that, and he needed to be sure, before he could rest, that Nadi was indeed one of the dead, and that the proper things were done for him for burial.

That is the spirit of the Egypt that I know. For a young man to travel over Egyptian roads more than one hundred miles in the night, in order to find his friend and identify his remains so that the grieving family would not be required to do it, and so that Nadi could be buried in the family tomb within the twenty four hours that the law required, was a gift of love for Nadi and for all of us who cared for him.

Ensha'allah.

Printed in the United States
210645BV00003B/112/P